Liondale English Language Series

Volume 1

IØ155739

Grammar and vocabulary practice
for intermediate and advanced students

Marc Loewenthal

Includes subscription to interactive materials on
www.eflworksheets.com

Liondale Publications
132A Heather Park Drive
Wembley
Middlesex HA0 1SN
United Kingdom
www.eflworksheets.com
subs@eflworksheets.com

Liondale English Language Series Volume 1
Grammar and vocabulary practice for intermediate and advanced students

ISBN 978-0-9558484-1-4

Free subscription to interactive activities on website included in purchase

The purchase of this book gives you an automatic subscription to extra interactive exercises on our website, www.eflworksheets.com. To claim your subscription, just email subs@eflworksheets.com, and you will receive a reply requesting some information from the book. Simply reply with the required information, and you will receive an identity and password to access the interactive materials. These materials can be used on one only computer at a time by one user. They may not be stored, amended, reproduced or transmitted in any other form or by any other means, electronic or mechanical, including multiple photocopying and recording, or by any other information storage or retrieval systems, other than that specified here, without prior written permission from the publisher.

Introduction

This book is the first in a series of books exploring aspects of grammar, vocabulary, pronunciation and spelling which are often neglected by standard textbooks, grammar books and vocabulary practice books. For example, some exercises in the Grammar section look at familiar grammar, such as Simple and Continuous tenses, in such a way as to get the learner to review what s/he knows already and explore it further. Other grammar exercises look at specific areas of grammar, such as the use of articles with days of the week, which the learner may not have noticed or considered before, but which need to be mastered for the learner to be a competent user of the language.

Apart from the Grammar section there are four others. The Vocabareas section looks at ways of practising and expanding vocabulary through collocation, affixation, categorisation and word formation. The Word Focus section practises in detail the meanings and usage of particular common words, such as *hand*, *hold* and *life*, particularly in phrases and common expressions. The Word Groups section practises literal and extended meanings of vocabulary based around a central theme, such as money, weather or numbers. The Wordplays section practises skills, such as spelling and proofreading, through exercises which involve searching for words with a letter missing or with an extra letter. It also aims to increase vocabulary building through word puzzles and wordplays.

These exercises are intended both for classroom use and for self study. They are particularly useful for teachers to follow up grammar or vocabulary which has been presented and practised in the classroom. Equally, self-motivated students can use them for self-study by reading the notes for each activity first and then checking the answers after they have finished. Other volumes to come in this series will also focus on the above themes. If you find these materials useful and enjoyable, we hope you will welcome the new volumes when they come out.

Our website, www.eflworksheets.com, has over ninety free materials for downloading and printing, along with exercises which are completed online. It also has a password protected section with interactive exercises based on the exercises in this book, and the purchase of this book gives you an automatic subscription to these materials. The online materials have additional explanations and feedback on each of the exercises, so they can reinforce and consolidate what the students learn from doing the exercises in this book. To claim your subscription, just email subs@eflworksheets.com, and you will receive a reply requesting some information from the book. Simply reply with the required information and you will receive an identity and password to access the interactive materials at any time you wish.

GRAMMAR

This section consists of twenty exercises which either explore aspects of grammar not always covered in standard grammar books, or extend more basic grammar. It is recommended that students practise these aspects of grammar in class and do these exercises as extension and consolidation activities. Teachers should ensure that students look through the notes for each exercise before tackling it.

Contents

Grammar Notes

1. *Would*: future or past?

One of the most common uses of *would* is to denote hypothetical and unlikely situations in the present and future:

a. *What would you do if you won the lottery? Would you give me some money?*

However, it is also used to denote events and situations in the past which happened regularly, much like *used to*:

b. *When I was young, my father would take me to watch the local football team every Saturday.*

This exercise is designed to help the learner distinguish between the two uses. In some cases, either use is possible, but one is more likely than the other. This will be indicated in the answers where necessary.

2. Double passives

Verbs which take an object can usually be used in the passive:

The witness saw three men running from the bank. → Three men were seen running from the bank (by the witness).

Verbs which take two objects can have two passives:

a. *Some people gave money to the beggar. → Money was given to the beggar (by some people).*
b. *Some people gave the beggar money. → The beggar was given money (by some people).*

In these examples, the passive sentence *b.* is more natural in everyday speech than sentence *a.* This exercise practises the formation of passive sentences like this with other verbs which take double objects.

3. Present tense oppositions: Simple or Continuous?

In English, there is usually a difference between the Simple and Continuous tenses, whether Present, Past or Perfect. This activity practises the main oppositions between the Present Simple and Present Continuous:

- Usually vs. Now: *I drink coffee - I'm drinking coffee.*
- Permanent vs. Temporary: *I live by myself - I'm living with my parents.*

- Regular vs. One-time (future reference): *The train leaves at 10.00 - I'm leaving at 10.00.*
- Normal schedule vs. Altered schedule: *The train leaves at 10.00 - The 10.00 train is leaving at 10.30.*

4. Past tense oppositions: Simple, Perfect or Continuous?

In English, there is usually a difference between the Simple, Continuous and Perfect tenses, whether Present, Past or Future. This activity practises the main oppositions between the Past Simple, Past Continuous and Past Perfect:

- One action follows another: *When I got home (1), everyone ate (2).*
- One action happens during another: *When I got home, everyone was eating (they started before I got home).*
- One action happens after another is completed: *When I got home (2), everyone had eaten (1).*

Sometimes one or other of the tenses can be used, depending on the situation. If it is clear which action happened first, the Past Perfect is not necessary:

a. *After I finished/had finished my homework, I watched a film.*

In some cases either the Past Simple or the Past Continuous can be used if both actions continue together or if it is not necessary to specify one action which happens after the other started. All of these basically mean the same:

b. *He sang while he worked.*
c. *He was singing while he was working.*
d. *He sang while he was working.*
e. *He was singing while he worked.*

Either the Past Simple or the Past Continuous can be used to refer to an action over a prolonged time if the completion or result is not specified: *I worked all night. I was working all night.*

5. Present and Perfect tense oppositions: Simple or Continuous?

In English, there is usually a difference between the Simple and Continuous tenses, whether Present, Past or Perfect. This activity practises the main oppositions between the Present Continuous, the Present Perfect Simple and the Present Perfect Continuous.

The Present Perfect tenses always relate a present situation with a past one in some way. Usually, with the Present Perfect Simple and Continuous, the difference is between an action which started in the past and is now completed, as in sentence a., and an action which started in the past and is not yet finished, as in sentence b.:

a. *I've cleaned the kitchen. Let's have dinner.*
b. *I've been cleaning the kitchen for the last hour, but there's still a lot to do.*

The Present Continuous is often used with the Present Perfect Simple if an action is not yet complete:

c. *John hasn't left work yet; he's still working.*

The Present Perfect Continuous is usually only used to describe an action in progress if the duration of that action is emphasised:

d. *I'm working in the centre of town. I've been working there for over a month now.*

Sometimes the Present Perfect Continuous is used to show the present result of a past action:

e. *Look how dirty you are! Have you been playing in the garden again?*

Sometimes there is little difference between the Present Perfect Simple and Continuous if there is no obvious completion to the action:

f. *I've waited/been waiting for a bus for over an hour, but nothing's arrived.*

However, this is not true if there is an expected completion to the action:

g. *I've been cooking dinner for over an hour, but I haven't finished yet.*

but not:

h. *I've cooked dinner for over an hour, but I haven't finished yet.*

In g., there is an expected time when the cooking is completed, whereas in f. there is no obvious point where the waiting is completed, while h. is not normal usage.

6. Relative clauses: defining or non-defining?

In English there are two basic types of relative clause: defining and non-defining. A defining relative clause distinguishes one thing/person/idea from another. A non-defining relative clause simply adds extra information without distinguishing a thing/person/idea from another. Look at these examples:

- Defining: *The teacher who helped me the most at school was my history teacher.*
- Non-defining: *The teacher, who left the classroom for five minutes, came back and found the children fighting.*

In the defining clause, the speaker has more than one teacher in mind and defines the one who helped him/her the most as the history teacher. In the non-defining clause, there is only one teacher, and that teacher left the class and returned to find the children fighting.

Here are some more examples:

- Defining: *The teacher who was suspended was the geography teacher.*
- Non-defining: *The headmaster, who was giving his weekly address to the students, emphasised the importance of responsibility.*

In the defining clause there are a number of teachers who could be suspended and the one in question is the geography teacher. In the non-defining clause, there is only one headmaster and he gave a talk about responsibility.

Some important points are:

- Defining clauses never use commas to separate them from the main clause. Non-defining clauses always use commas to separate them from the main clause.
- When spoken, defining relative clauses have no pauses. Non-defining relative clauses usually have a pause where the commas are.
- Defining relative clauses are very common, especially in speech. Non-defining clauses are usually used in more formal, written language.

7. Relative clauses: omitting the pronoun

In defining relative clauses, the pronoun - *who, which, that* - can be omitted from the sentence if it is the object of the verb, or if it is with a preposition, but not if it is the subject:

a. *The man (who) I saw outside my house was the same one who stole my car.*
b. *The plane (which) we flew home on was the same one (that) we had flown out on.*

In *a.* the first relative pronoun *who* is the object of the verb *saw*, so it can be omitted, but the second pronoun *who* is the subject of the verb *stole*, so it cannot be omitted. In *b.* the first pronoun *which* goes with the preposition *on*, and the second pronoun *that* also goes with the preposition *on*, so they can both be omitted, which is usually the case in everyday spoken English.

8. Preposition choices

Certain prepositions of place and motion have similar meanings, which can present problems for learners when choosing the most appropriate one for a particular situation. These in particular can be problematic:

- *over* contrasts with *under*, and both usually indicate an exact position (*a.* and *b.*), while *above* contrasts with *below* (*c.* and *d.*), and both usually simply indicate the relative level rather than the exact position.

a. *My bedroom is over the kitchen*
b. *The kitchen is under my bedroom*
c. *The memorial is on a hill above the city.*
d. *The village sits in a valley below the mountain.*

- When they are used to indicate motion, *over* and *under* usually indicate linear movement, e.g. from one side to the other (*e.* and *f.*), while *above* and *below* usually indicate non-linear movement, or movement in no particular direction (*g.* and *h.*).

e. *The plane flew over the house.*
f. *The car drove under the bridge.*
g. *Planes fly above the ground.*
h. *These trains run below the ground.*

The following prepositions are also used:

- *across* indicates movement from one side to the other, or a position on one side from another. *I walked across the road. I live across the city from my office.*
- *past* indicates position on the other side of a place, or movement to that position. *My house is just past the cinema. I walked past the stadium.*
- *beyond* is similar to *past*, but usually indicates a position further away. *Beyond the mountains lies a huge desert. He has never travelled beyond the mountains.*
- *through* indicates position or movement to the other side of an enclosed area. *The village is through the tunnel on the other side. I never drive through the city because of all the traffic.*
- *along* Indicates a further position or movement in one direction. *My house is along this road. I walked along the path deeper into the woods.*

9. Multi-function replacements 1
10. Multi-function replacements 2

Some words can function as one part of speech or another, and their meaning depends on the way they are used. For example, *cross* can be a noun, adjective or verb, and its meaning varies with each function. The idea of a multi-function replacement is that in each function the word can be replaced by another word or phrase with a similar meaning. Look at these examples:

a. *You should find a safe place to* **cross** *the road.* Replacement: <u>go over</u> (verb)
b. *In front of the church they erected a large* **cross**. Replacement: <u>symbol of Christianity</u> (noun)
c. *When my mother saw the broken window, she was very* **cross**. Replacement: <u>angry</u> (adjective)

These exercises practise uses and meanings of some common words which can function as two or more parts of speech, such as noun + verb, noun + adjective, verb + adjective, noun + verb + adjective, noun + verb + adjective + adverb.

<u>11. Nouns: countable or uncountable? 1</u>
<u>12. Nouns: countable or uncountable? 2</u>

Some nouns in English are exclusively or almost always countable: *table, idea, telephone, person.* Countable nouns must have a determiner in the singular: *a, the, this, that etc,* and are also used in the plural.

Other nouns are exclusively or almost always uncountable: *information, advice, money, milk, air.* Uncountable nouns are never used with the indefinite article *a,* and don't take the plural.

However, there are many nouns which can be countable – C, or uncountable - U. Some of them have very similar meanings whether they are C or U, and others have quite different meanings. Look at these examples:

a. *I want to write a letter. Have you got any* **paper**? – U
b. *This is a really difficult exam. I have to do three different* **papers**. - C

c. *I'm sorry. I can't help you at the moment. I've got too much* **work**. – U
d. *Look at this book I've just bought. It's the complete* **works** *of Shakespeare.* - C

e. *We need a new manager with five years'* **experience** *of this type of work.* - U
f. *I did a parachute jump last week. It was a fantastic* **experience**! - C

g. *I love being in the country in spring. Look at all those* **lambs**! - C
h. *We're having* **lamb** *for dinner tonight. Would you like some?* - U

i. *I bought some* **eggs** *yesterday, but three of them were broken.* - C
j. *Look at your shirt. You've got* **egg** *all down the front!* – U

These exercises look at some of these common words and how they are used as countable and uncountable nouns.

13. Nouns: general or particular? 1
14. Nouns: general or particular? 2

There are many nouns in English which are used with or without articles, depending on whether the meaning is particular - P, or general - G. The use is similar to that of countable and uncountable nouns, in the sense that nouns used with a general meaning are usually singular and do not have any article or other determiner. When they are used in a particular sense, they can take an article or other determiner, or can be used in the plural. Look at these examples:

a. *Foreign affairs are a very important part of **government**. - G*
b. *The **government** has decided to raise taxes to 30%. - P*

c. *My new house has three bedrooms and a **study** where I can work in peace. - P*
d. *I've decided to take a break from my **studies** and travel for a year. – P*
e. *You should try to do at least three hours of **study** every day if you want to pass your exams. – G*

f. *Scientists have sent a new spaceship to Mars in an attempt to find **life**. - G*
g. *My father had a very happy and exciting **life**. - P*
h. *Three people lost their **lives** in the train crash. - P*

i. *If you take this course, you will learn some very useful office **skills**, like typing and filing. - P*
j. *You need a lot of **skill** to fly a helicopter in a strong wind. - G*

15. Two-form adverbs 1
16. Two-form adverbs 2

Most adverbs are formed from adjectives with the suffix *-ly*, e.g.: *beautiful - beautifully, strange - strangely, nice - nicely*. However, there is a group of common adverbs which have two forms, one with and one without *-ly*, each with a different meaning. These include the following:

a. *I eat food from all over the world, but I like Italian food **most**.*
b. *Tomorrow there will be snow, **mostly** on higher ground.*

c. *The plane flew **high** over the city, leaving a long vapour trail.*
d. *I talked to your teacher about your work. He says it's excellent. He thinks very **highly** of you.*

This exercise practises some of these important adverbs.

17. -ing forms: Gerund, Continuous, Participle or Adjective?

The -ing ending in English can have a variety of uses:

- Gerund/verbal noun - *I like **reading** horror stories and I'm keen on **playing** football.*
- Continuous tenses - *I can't come out tonight. I'm **studying** for my exams.*
- Present participle - *He sat in a café, **drinking** coffee and **watching** the world go by.*
- Adjective - *I read a really **interesting** book last week, but the one I'm reading now is the most **boring** book I've ever read.*

This exercise practises identifying these forms with the aim of enabling learners to distinguish between them.

18. Articles with days of the week

Much of the time that we use the days of the week, we don't use an article with them. However, there are times when either of the articles, *a* or *the*, is used with them to indicate either a specified day or an unspecified day. Look at these examples:

a. *I'll see you on Sunday.* This is the Sunday following the time that I'm speaking.
b. *I'll see you on the Sunday.* This is a Sunday at a particular time in the future that I'm talking about, for example, during a holiday.
c. *I'll see you on a Sunday.* This is some unspecified Sunday some time in the future.

d. *I saw them on Sunday.* This is the most recent Sunday before the time I am speaking.
e. *I saw them on the Sunday.* This is a Sunday at a particular time in the past that I'm talking about, for example, during a holiday.
f. *I saw them on a Sunday.* This is some unspecified Sunday at some time in the past.

This exercise gives learners practice in distinguishing between situations when we need to use an article with days of the week or not.

19. Verbs with or without prepositions 1
20. Verbs with or without prepositions 2

There are many verbs in English which can be used with or without a following preposition, in some cases with different prepositions, and usually with a different meaning, e.g.:

a. You shouldn't **believe** everything you read in the newspapers.
b. I don't **believe in** ghosts. I think they're just your imagination.

c. Remember. When the lawyer asks you questions, you need to **answer** them honestly and clearly.
d. You've got quite a lot of freedom in your job, but make sure you don't make any bad decisions, or you'll have to **answer to** me.

These exercises help learners decide when to include a preposition and when not to.

1. *Would*: future or past?

Read the sentences below and decide if they refer to the future or the past, or possibly either, depending on the context. Write F (future), P (past) or E (either) in the space at the end of each sentence.

1. You look really tired and run down. You've been working far too hard. I'd take a long holiday if I were you. _____

2. We'd always play chess indoors if it was raining. _____ That's why I'm such a good chess player today.

3. I haven't seen my cousin John for months. If he visited me now, I'd take him straight out for a meal. _____

4. This house is far too small for my family now, but I can't afford a bigger one. I'd buy a much bigger house if I won the lottery. _____

5. In the winter it would snow quite a lot. _____ Nowadays, though, the temperature rarely gets below freezing point.

6. I used to do a lot of winter sports as a child and I still do. It would be lovely if it snowed in winter so we could go skiing. _____

7. I've always enjoyed having you round to my house. It would be nice if you could come to visit me more often. _____

8. I know you've got a lot of work to do and I would love to help you if I had more time. _____

9. I've always enjoyed cooking. I would help my grandmother make cakes if she was visiting. _____

10. We would go abroad on holiday if we had enough money. _____ The trouble is it's always been so expensive.

11. The government would pass as many laws as it could if it had enough votes in parliament. _____

12. If the government were more organised, it would be able to pass as many laws as it wanted. _____

2. Double passives

Read the sentences and choose a verb and an object from the each of the two lists below to complete them. Remember to put the verb in an appropriate tense and form of the passive.

Verbs	Objects
bring, hand, leave, loan, offer, owe, pay, promise, refuse, send	a replacement, over £1m, an email, our meals, the other half, too little, entry, a saloon car, double time, an envelope

1. I wanted to sell my car at the auction today, but I _____

   _____ for it, well below the real value of the car, so I didn't sell.

2. When the spy asked for the money for the secret plans, he _____

   _____ with £10,000 in it.

3. The service at the restaurant was terrible. We _____

   _____ by the waiter an hour after we ordered and they were cold.

4. The boys tried to get into the night club, but they _____

   _____ because none of them could prove they were over eighteen.

5. Marion's really lucky. Her rich aunt died last month and, as her favourite niece,

   she _____ _____ in the will.

6. I'm really angry with the car hire company. We _____

   _____ when we booked, but they gave us a smaller one on the

   day.

7. My boss says, if I work over the weekend to finish the new computer project, I

   _____ _____, so I'm going to do it.

8. So far I've received half the money for the work I did, so _____ still

   _____ _____, and I expect to get it next week.

9. The garage couldn't fix my car in time for my trip, so I _____

   _____ till next week. It's really nice, much better than mine.

10. Don't worry about missing the meeting. You _____

    _____ straight after the meeting with all the minutes attached.

3. Present tense oppositions: Simple or Continuous?

Choose one of the verbs from the list to put into each space in the sentences below. Make sure you put them in the appropriate tense and form, and put any bracketed adverbs and negatives in the correct place.

answer, arrive (2), come, fly, hope, leave (3), live, meet, run, save, say, see, start, stay, study, take, think (3), watch, work (4)

1. I usually _____ at the office, but today I _____ at home, as the trains _____ (not) because of the transport strike.

2. I'm really fed up with Jim. He's so lazy that you can never rely on him. He (always) _____ breaks when he should _____.

3. I _____ to Australia next Saturday. My flight _____ at 10.00 in the evening and _____ at 6.00 in the morning two days later.

4. If I _____ my favourite TV programme at home in the evening and the phone _____, I (never) _____ it.

5. Saturday's big game _____ at 3.00, so I _____ my house at 2.00 and _____ the others at the entrance to the stadium.

6. There's been a delay, so the 2.15 train to Edinburgh (now) _____ at 2.45. I _____ we _____ in Edinburgh on time.

7. My husband (always) _____ late at the office these days, or at least that's what he _____. _____ you _____ he _____ another woman?

8. I _____ about buying a new car, but I'm not sure what to get. I _____ I'll go along to a few showrooms and have a good look.

9. I don't have a place of my own at the moment. I _____ with my parents until I _____ enough money to buy a flat.

10. John (not) _____ out with us tonight as he _____ for his exams. In fact, he _____ in every night this week.

4. Past tense oppositions: Simple, Perfect or Continuous?

Choose one of the verbs from the list to put into each space in the sentences below. Make sure you put them in the appropriate tense and form, and put any bracketed adverbs and negatives in the correct place. In some cases two answers are possible.

arrive(2), be (2), buy, dance, drive, finish (2), get, eat, go (2), happen, have, hear, intend, know, lie, put, rain, relax, see (4), tell, try, walk

1. When I _____ home yesterday after a long day's work, there _____ no dinner left as everyone _____ it all.

2. We _____ in the garden when we _____ a terrible noise in the street. There _____ a terrible accident.

3. After I _____ all my work, I _____ out to a nightclub with some friends. We _____ all night to some really great music.

4. When we _____ at my grandfather's, he _____ in bed. I (never) _____ him so ill. I was really worried about him.

5. I _____ along the beach when I _____ a boy in the sea screaming for help, but nobody _____ to help him.

6. When I _____ up in the morning, it _____ hard outside. Luckily I _____ the washing in the night before.

7. I _____ to go on holiday last week, but we (suddenly) _____ a lot of work, so I _____ it off till next week.

8. John _____ me that he _____ a brand new car, but when I _____ him in the street, he _____ his old one.

9. As soon as I _____ my last exam at university, I _____ straight out of the exam hall to the bar to celebrate.

10. As soon as I _____ the ambulance outside my parents' house, I _____ that something terrible _____.

5. Perfect tense oppositions: Simple or Continuous?

Choose one of the verbs from the list to put into each space in the sentences below. Make sure you put them in the appropriate tense and form, and put any bracketed adverbs and negatives in the correct place. In some cases two answers are possible.

answer, call, date (2), decide, eat, expect, finish, get, have, hear (3), leave (2), paint (3), shine, snow, think, work

1. I _____ a lot of good things about you and your voice, and now that I _____ your singing, I can see that it's true.

2. I _____ this room all day and I _____ really tired. I'm going to take a break and finish decorating it later.

3. So far I _____ three of the five rooms and I _____ the fourth now, so I've still got two to go.

4. Do you know where Jenny is? I _____ her five times today on her mobile phone, but she _____ at all. I'm getting concerned.

5. I _____ a lot about your application for the sales manager's position and I _____ to give you the job. You can start on Monday.

6. Why is it that you (still) _____ your dinner? Why (not) _____ it yet? We need to leave now to get to the theatre on time.

7. What a great day for skiing! The sun _____ and it _____. Look at all that beautiful fresh snow! Let's go out now.

8. I can't believe Rachel (still) _____ Geoff. They _____ for over a month and she _____ (not) him yet. He's such an awful man. I don't know what she sees in him.

9. Welcome to London! I _____ you for some time, and now you're here at last. I hope you _____ a good journey.

10. _____ you _____ the news about the new manager? He _____ (not) here for more than a month, but he _____ his job already. I wonder why he decided to go.

6. Relative clauses: defining or non-defining?

Read these sentences and decide if they are defining or non-defining. If you think a clause is defining, then put one or two commas in the correct places to mark it off from the main clause. Defining clauses have no commas.

1. People who don't pay their taxes make it more difficult for everyone else.

2. The Prime Minister who is visiting China this week has signed a new trade agreement.

3. All the tourists who were injured in the coach crash were taken to hospital. The others were flown back home last night.

4. The audience who had waited over an hour for the concert to begin demanded their money back.

5. Another minister has resigned from the government which is now dangerously close to falling.

6. The leader of the opposition who accused the Prime Minister of abusing his position called for a new election as soon as possible.

7. Our manager is the sort of boss who doesn't want to listen to any criticism of his methods.

8. After the game the losing team complained of having to play three times in five days which had left them absolutely exhausted.

9. A university is a place where students have the chance to learn to live on their own and take care of themselves.

10. The hostages from the hijack were freed by the police and taken to the Central Park Hotel where they were reunited with their families.

11. My son is really pleased. He managed to get a place at London University which was the first choice on his application form.

12. London was the university which my son really wanted to get into and he's really happy that they accepted him.

7. Relative clauses: omitting the pronoun

Read through these sentences, which contain defining relative clauses. Decide which relative pronouns can be left out and delete them where appropriate. Take care, since in some cases *who*, *where* and *that* are not used as relative pronouns.

1. I'm worried about Harry. He's changed so much. He's just not the man who I married.

2. What happened about that job that you applied for? Did you get it?

3. Are you sure that Jenny said that? She's not the sort of person who would gossip about you and say such horrible things.

4. Our flat is just far too small now. I'm looking for a large, detached house where all the children can have their own bedrooms.

5. We went skiing over the Christmas holiday. It was lovely. The hotel which we stayed in laid on a really great party for New Year.

6. The only person who I'd give everything up for is my wife.

7. When I told Jenny that she had passed all her exams, she didn't say anything. That wasn't exactly the type of reaction that I had expected.

8. That's the job that I'd love to do, that I'd drop my current job for tomorrow.

9. Is there anyone here who can speak Russian? I can't understand anything that this customer's saying.

10. There are so many things that I could say about the book that I don't know where to start.

11. The thing which really annoys me about Frank is the way that he talks to other people, as if he were better than them.

12. I don't believe it! I ordered a new computer, but the one which has been delivered is not the one which I ordered.

13. The hotel which we stayed in on this holiday was far better than the one where we stayed last year.

14. The car which is parked outside Pete's house isn't the same one which Pete bought last week.

15. I'd like to know who you think is the best teacher who ever taught you.

8. Preposition choices

Choose one of these prepositions to fill the gap in each sentence. In some cases more than one preposition is possible.

above, across, along, below, beyond, over, past, through, under

1. The best way to get to the motorway is to go _____ this road for a kilometre, then _____ the river and take the first right.
2. The space probe Voyager 1 flew _____ the planet Jupiter and eventually travelled _____ the boundaries of the solar system.
3. We had a really nice flight. We flew _____ so many islands, which were spread out _____ us, though before we landed, we had to fly around _____ the city a few times because of the air traffic.
4. The Mount Everest base camp is around 5500 metres _____ sea level, and about 3500 metres _____ the summit.
5. What really annoys me is when I'm sitting and reading my newspaper and someone is also trying to read it _____ my shoulder.
6. There are two ways you can get _____ the river. There's the tunnel _____ it and further down there's a bridge _____ it.
7. We slept up on the mountain and when we woke up the view was fantastic. The whole valley was _____ us and _____ the river we could see the castle.
8. The last part of the walk _____ the hills was the most dangerous part. There were many large potholes in the ground and we had to be careful not to fall _____ any of them.
9. There's a lovely new Italian restaurant near here. It's just _____ the road _____ the post office.
10. If you need a roof _____ your head, you can stay at my house for a few days. You'll find the key either _____ the mat or _____ the door.

9. Multi-function replacements 1

This exercise focuses on these three words: *round*, *back* and *still*. Choose one of the words or phrases in the list with a meaning close to the meaning of the focus word in the sentence. Indicate also what part of speech the word is: n. (noun), v. (verb), adj. (adjective), adv. (adverb), p. (preposition).

again, alcohol-making apparatus, calm down, circular, here and there, in the past, motionless, near, rear, stage, support, up to now

1.   I'm not going to work today. I've hurt my *back* _____ and I need to rest it.

2.   I can't believe that you're *still* _____ in bed! You're so lazy! Get up!

3.   We need to get some petrol. Can you ask that man if there's a petrol station *round* _____ here?

4.   The weather was lovely this morning when I woke up. The air was completely *still* _____. There wasn't any wind at all.

5.   We had a really lovely holiday in Spain last year. The area was beautiful and the hotel was excellent. I'd love to go *back* _____.

6.   Jane's going *round* _____ telling everyone that she's getting married, but I've never met her boyfriend.

7.   Roger has set up a *still* _____ in his garden shed so he can make his own whisky.

8.   I remember *back* _____ when I was a boy I used to climb over the farmer's wall and steal his apples. It was great fun!

9.   It's fantastic that our team has reached the third *round* _____ of the competition, but I can't see us getting to the final and winning the cup.

10.   The people were shaking their fists, shouting and jeering angrily, but they *stilled* _____ when their leader got up to speak.

11.   Scientists long ago found out that the earth isn't exactly *round* _____, but is actually slightly wider at the equator.

12.   If Heather stands for the position of president of the students' union, I'm going to *back* _____ her. I'm sure she'll win.

10. Multi-function replacements 2

This exercise focuses on these four words: *bar, fast, just* and *too*. Choose one of the words or phrases in the list with a meaning close to the meaning of the focus word in the sentence. Indicate also what part of speech the word is: c (conjunction), n. (noun), v. (verb), adj. (adjective), adv. (adverb).

also, barrier, drinking place, eat nothing, except, excessively, fair, only, quick, rod, stop, tightly

1. You can't *bar* _____ me from entering. I've been a member of this club for over ten years. I want to see the manager!

2. I buy property, fix it up and sell it on after a couple of months. It's a good way to make a lot of *fast* _____ money.

3. Police have found a metal *bar* _____, which they think was used in the murder of the actress Karen Brown last week.

4. Can you do me a favour? I have to go out, so can you look after the children? I'll be gone for *just* _____ an hour or so.

5. You'll have to stop at the entrance to the car park because there's a *bar* _____ across it. Call the security to open it.

6. You can't go and see that film. It's *too* _____ violent.

7. I can arrange to meet you any day this month *bar* _____ the 20th, as that's my sister's wedding day.

8. I usually eat far too much over Christmas, so I *fast* _____ for a couple of days just to get back to normal.

9. I'm really thirsty. After we check into the hotel, let's go down to the *bar* _____ for a few beers.

10. Not only did I pass all my exams, but I got the top mark in the class *too* _____.

11. I tried to pull the key out of the lock, but it was stuck *fast* _____, so I had to call the locksmith to get it out.

12. The judge awarded Maureen $100,000 as a *just* _____ settlement for the injuries she had suffered in the accident.

11. Nouns: countable or uncountable? 1

Choose one of these words to put into each gap in the sentences. Each word is used once as a countable noun (C) and once as an uncountable noun (U). Indicate how the noun is used with C or U. Make sure you put each uncountable noun in the correct form, with an article or in the plural.

business, colour, glass, noise, room, wood

1. These new aquariums aren't made of _____, but of a special new unbreakable type of plastic.
2. Spring is my favourite time of the year because it brings back _____ after the drabness of winter.
3. I've decided to leave my job and start up _____. I've saved over £10,000 and the bank's lent me another £20,000.
4. I buy all my furniture from Tradefair Furniture because they only use _____ which is sourced from sustainable forests.
5. Listen! Did you hear _____ outside in the garden? I think there's someone trying to break in.
6. We've booked _____ at the Excelsior Hotel for our holiday. It's the best hotel in the town.
7. Are you doing the washing up? Be careful with those wine _____. They cost a lot of money.
8. I've decided not to do _____ with Andrew's company because I don't think they can supply what I need. I'll have to find another supplier.
9. Let's walk over the hill and down into the valley. There's _____ there where we can have a picnic under the trees.
10. On the day of the big football match the streets were full of football fans dressed in the _____ of their favourite team.
11. Sorry. You'll have to take the bus. I haven't got enough _____ in the car to take everyone to the party.
12. Can you shut the window? There's a lot of _____ from the traffic outside and I'm trying to study.

12. Nouns: countable or uncountable? 2

Choose one of these words to put into each gap in the sentences. Each word is used once as a countable noun (C) and once as an uncountable noun (U). Indicate how the noun is used with C or U. Make sure you put each uncountable noun in the correct form, with an article or in the plural.

activity, bite, cold, death, experience, value

1. I've applied for a new job, but I'm not sure that I can get it. They're looking for someone with lots of _____.

2. When it gets as hot as it is today, we don't get much _____ in the office because people start to get tired and lazy. Some of them even sleep.

3. The team hasn't been playing well at all. They need to show far more _____ and enthusiasm in the second half.

4. There's been a train crash on the main line. Thankfully, there have been no _____ reported, but twenty people were injured.

5. That's the trouble with this time of the year. There are so many viruses going round that many people get _____ and pass them on to others.

6. If you want to buy a new car, you really have to look around to get good _____ for money these days.

7. I don't like the look of that dog. It looks quite fierce. Be careful or it might give you _____.

8. My children love going to summer camp. They make lots of friends and have lots of fun _____ to do every day, like swimming and climbing.

9. _____, and not lack of food, is the biggest killer of birds in winter, especially when the temperature reaches below zero.

10. Travelling round the world was one of the best things I've ever done. I've had lots of fantastic _____ with people in so many different places.

11. Even though I'm getting quite old, I'm not really afraid of _____. I'm ready to face it when it comes.

12. You have to remember that people in other countries may have different _____ to the ones we have, and you have to respect them.

13. Nouns: general or particular? 1

The following words can be used in either a general sense (G), without definite or indefinite article, or a particular sense (P), with an article. Each of them is used twice, once with and once without an article.

choice, conversation, culture, democracy, shame, taste

1. What parents want in education today is _____, and our party is the only one which can deliver it to all parents.
2. Every country which joins the European Union has to be _____. It's a basic requirement for membership.
3. The problem people have these days is they don't communicate enough. In the old days _____ was an important part of everyday life.
4. In South East Asia people eat a fruit called durian, which has _____ unlike any other fruit you'll ever eat. It's completely unique.
5. It is generally agreed that _____ which has contributed the most to European civilisation was that of Rome.
6. People in positions of authority used to resign out of _____ and take the blame if they failed, but nowadays this rarely happens.
7. The first people to introduce _____ as a political system were the ancient Athenians.
8. I had _____ with your teacher today about your work and he told me that you have to study harder if you're going to pass your exams.
9. If I had to make _____ between football and golf, it would have to be football, always.
10. Steven really has got _____. He only buys the best quality clothes and dines out in top restaurants.
11. It really is _____ that you have to leave today. I was hoping we could go out together for a nice meal tonight.
12. _____ is a very important part of human identity. It defines who we are, where we belong and how we live our lives.

14. Nouns: general or particular? 2

The following words can be used in either a general sense (G), without definite or indefinite article, or a particular sense (P), with an article. Each of them is used twice, once with and once without an article.

competition, discipline, dress, judgement, promise, purpose

1. If you want to succeed in life you must have _____. Without it people waste their time and don't do their work as well as they should.

2. Today was the last day in the divorce case between the actor Jimmy Cannon and his wife. _____ is expected tomorrow.

3. _____ is an important part of a person's culture. What you wear can help define who you are and what social groups you belong to.

4. Your son is showing _____ in his work and I expect him to pass all his exams if he continues in the same way.

5. _____ of the clutch in a car is to allow the driver to change gear in order to increase and decrease speed.

6. In any top sports club there's a lot of _____ for places in the team. It's a very healthy situation.

7. My wife usually wears _____ to work, but today she decided to wear a trouser suit.

8. Do you like my new car? I won it in _____. It was the first prize.

9. I made _____ to my son that I'd buy him a car if he passed his final exams. He passed with three top grades, so here's the car.

10. When you have so many choices in life, it's important to think carefully and exercise _____. Otherwise, you might make the wrong choice.

11. Yoga is _____ which requires a lot of hard work and dedication if you are to do it well.

12. The climb was particularly difficult because of the bad weather, but the team showed _____ and that's how they managed to get to the summit.

15. Two-form adverbs 1

Choose the correct adverb from the list and fill the space in each sentence. Each adverb is used once with the suffix -*ly* and once without. Make sure you adjust the spelling where necessary.

close, fine, high, just, sharp, wrong

1. I left the house in plenty of time to get to the airport, but there was an accident on the way. Luckily, I arrived _____ in time.

2. My children went into my neighbour's garden to get their football. She was very angry and spoke very _____ to them.

3. We stayed at a forest camp where they have a walkway _____ up in the trees so that you can see the wildlife close up. The kids really loved it.

4. Children! Be careful! Don't go too _____ to the cliff edge. It's very dangerous. You might fall.

5. Do you really want to leave for the airport at 6.00? That's cutting it a bit _____. The flight leaves at 7.15 and it's twenty miles away.

6. Patricia was allowed to take the exam again after she was _____ accused of cheating in the first one. It turned out that someone had copied from her.

7. The boxer Julius Frost was found guilty of causing death by dangerous driving and _____ sentenced to five years in prison.

8. It's up to you to be here on time, or you'll miss the coach. We're leaving at 8 o'clock _____, and we're not waiting for anyone.

9. Sorry. Is your phone number 259987, or 255987? Oh, so it's 255987. I must have heard you _____ the first time you told me.

10. Detective Smith picked up the gun and looked at it _____, trying to see if it had been fired.

11. I'm looking forward to working with the new manager. John worked with him before and speaks very _____ of him.

12. The tennis final was very _____ balanced until the last set, when Duckworth broke Atkinson's serve and won the match.

16. Two-form adverbs 2

Choose the correct adverb from the list and fill the space in each sentence. Each adverb is used once with the suffix -*ly* and once without. Make sure you adjust the spelling where necessary.

easy, free, hard, late, pretty, short

1. Thompson led the rally for most of the way but his car had a puncture only 1km _____ of the finish and he came in last.

2. I wouldn't go back to that restaurant. The food's very good but the service is _____ awful.

3. I must go to the gym more often. I've noticed that I've been putting on weight _____, though I haven't been eating more than usual.

4. The front door was stuck at first, so we had to push _____ to open it. Inside the flat there was a terrible mess.

5. You should have come to the game. Our team won _____, 5 - 0. The other team was really poor.

6. Are you coming to that new electrical store? They're giving away plasma televisions _____ to the first hundred customers.

7. This is your last warning. If you come to work _____ one more time, I'm afraid you'll lose your job.

8. Don't worry about what people think of you in this company. You can talk _____ about anything and people won't judge you.

9. Kevin wants to come out to the cinema with us. He'll be here _____ so let's get ready.

10. I really appreciate my holidays these days. It gives me a chance just to take it _____ for a few days and forget about work.

11. My daughter was so happy to be a bridesmaid at my sister's wedding. She was dressed really _____ and did everything so well.

12. The fog was so thick I could _____ see further than five metres in front of me.

17. -ing forms: Gerund, Continuous, Participle or Adjective?

Read through these sentences, put in the appropriate word from the list and decide which form of -ing it is. Write G, C, P or A in the space after the relevant form.

believing, crossing, going, interesting, inviting, joking, lying, lying, making, seeing, trying (2), working (2), worrying (3)

1. John's _____ _____ to cycle round the world in a year. Good luck to him. I hope he manages to do it.

2. John's so _____ _____. Every time I clean up the house he makes a mess and leaves it for me to clean up again. I get so annoyed!

3. Don't worry if you missed the lecture this morning. It wasn't very _____ _____. You can have a look at my notes if you want.

4. The thing I find difficult in this job is _____ _____ with a manager who can't do his job properly. It really affects how I do mine.

5. The government plans to provide more nursery places for the children of _____ _____ mothers so that they can organise their lives better.

6. I don't mind people _____ _____ mistakes but what really annoys me is _____ _____ to cover up them up. That's completely wrong.

7. When I opened the door, I found my grandmother _____ _____ on the floor. We called the doctor, but luckily, she wasn't hurt.

8. At first I thought that Steve was _____ _____ with me about buying a new Ferrari, but _____ _____ is _____ _____. He had really bought one, and it's really fantastic!

9. It's _____ _____ that there's so much traffic on the roads these days. It's so dangerous for children _____ _____ busy roads.

10. Tim's _____ _____ that he might not have passed his exams, but I told him that there was nothing more that he could do about it now.

11. There's no point in _____ _____ about what problems you might have twenty years from now. Think about today. That's what's important.

12. Do you fancy _____ _____ for a swim? The sea looks so warm and _____ _____. I can't wait to get in.

18. Articles with days of the week

Read these sentences and decide whether to put one of the articles *a* or *the* into the gap or leave it blank.

1. I'm going away on _____ Saturday, but I'll be back next week, probably on _____ Thursday or _____ Friday.
2. I had a lovely weekend in Paris last month. We took the train on _____ Friday afternoon and spent _____ Saturday touring the city.
3. I'm busy most Fridays but I can help you on _____ Saturday next month, or possibly _____ Sunday. I'll let you know when I'm free.
4. I've got the itinerary for the archaeological trip in July. When we arrive, we're meeting the Greek team on _____ Monday and travelling to the site on _____ Tuesday.
5. In my last job we usually had our staff meetings on _____ Wednesday, but sometimes we had them on _____ Thursday.
6. Sorry. Mavis isn't in today. She should be in tomorrow, or maybe _____ Thursday. I'll tell her to call you when I see her.
7. I was hoping to take _____ Friday off this week, but we've got a lot of work coming in, so I'll have to take _____ Friday off next month.
8. Did you go to the football match on _____ Saturday? I did. What a fantastic match! We won 4 – 0. It was _____ Saturday I'll never forget.
9. Which Wednesday would you prefer to meet on, _____ next Wednesday or _____ Wednesday after?
10. When I was a boy, the shops were open six days a week but never on _____ Sunday. They open every day now.
11. The happiest day in my life was _____ Saturday when I met my future wife. I'll always remember it. We fell in love at first sight.
12. I remember so much about my first day at work. It was _____ Monday when nothing seemed to go right.

19. Verbs with or without prepositions 1

Choose verbs from the box on the left and put them in the gaps in the sentences. Remember to put it in the correct tense and form. Each verb is used twice, once with and once without a preposition. Use each prepositions once only.

| apply, forget, know, see, start, watch | about, about, for, for, through, with |

1. I spent all day revising for my exams yesterday, but I _____ everything I learnt when I got into the exam room this morning.

2. OK then, we're all happy to go to a film tonight. I don't _____ Jim, but he usually likes going to a film, so we'll tell him when he comes.

3. Only half the class is here, but it's five past nine and I can't wait any longer. I'll have to _____ the lesson without them.

4. Let me introduce you to everyone. This is Ned. He works on the data from the telescope. He has to _____ any changes in the signal which might indicate intelligent life out there in the stars.

5. Alan tried to convince me that he was really sorry that he had taken my money, but I _____ him. I knew he wasn't really sorry.

6. I really want to _____ this job I found in the newspaper, but I'm not sure if I've got the right qualifications and experience.

7. Do you mean Alex? Yes, of course I _____ him. I used to play pool with him in the college bar. How is he doing now?

8. OK, everyone. This is going to be a long meeting and Joyce has to go early, so can we _____ item eight on the agenda? That's the most important one.

9. OK. Here's another hundred pounds, but I haven't _____ the other hundred I gave you last week, so you owe me £200 now.

10. If someone has a deep cut and it's bleeding quite a lot, take a clean cloth, cover the wound and _____ pressure to it.

11. I really need to talk to Carrie. Have you _____ her at all today?

12. The safari in Kenya was fantastic. We stayed in this tree house near the water hole, and we could _____ the animals coming and going.

20. Verbs with or without prepositions 2

Choose verbs from the box on the left and put them in the gaps in the sentences. Remember to put it in the correct tense and form. Each verb is used twice, once with and once without a preposition. Use each prepositions once only.

allow, arrange, buy, engage, hit, try	for, for, for, in, into, on

1. I'm sorry sir. We don't _____ smoking anywhere in the building. You'll have to go outside.

2. When you start driving remember to _____ first gear only after you put the clutch down. Otherwise, you'll stall the car.

3. After our flight was cancelled, the airline _____ us to stay in a really nice hotel till we left the next day.

4. After dinner the waiter brought us the dessert. It looked really nice, but when I _____ it, it tasted awful.

5. Our car broke down in the middle of the desert and we didn't know what to do. Then Tom _____ the idea of burning one of the tyres to make smoke so that rescuers could find us.

6. Guess what! Disney have _____ the rights to make my book into a film. I'm going to be rich!

7. I'm sorry. I just don't _____ this idea of Pete being the project leader. I'm just not convinced that he can handle the responsibility.

8. Jack's been arrested. The police say he was _____ importing tobacco and alcohol illegally.

9. We'll have to do all the financial calculations again. We didn't _____ the 1% increase in prices every year for the last ten years.

10. OK. Is everyone ready? Let's get into the car and _____ the road. Next stop, the south of France!

11. Now that Jenny's starting school in September, we've decided to _____ another baby. We'd love to have a boy.

12. There aren't enough people for us to hold the meeting today. We'll have to _____ another one for next week.

VOCABAREAS

This section consists of twenty exercises dealing with areas of vocabulary such as prefixation, suffixation, similar words and words linked semantically.

Contents

Notes on exercises

Vocabareas Notes

<u>1. Words with or without *a-*: adjective/adverb</u>
<u>2. Words with or without *a-*: noun - adverb</u>
<u>3. Words with or without *a-*: verb - adjective/adverb</u>

Some words in English can take a prefix *a-* (<u>not</u> the negative prefix *a-* as in *moral - amoral*), which can change the meaning of the word in various ways, depending on the type of word. In most cases it also changes the part of speech.

Exercise 1 practises adjectives and adverbs of this type. The adjectives are known as predicative, which means that they can not go before a noun, and usually follow the verb *to be* and various other verbs.

Exercise 2 practises adverbs which are formed from nouns and Exercise 3 practises predicative adjectives and adverbs which are formed from verbs.

<u>4. Negative prefixes 1</u>
<u>5. Negative prefixes 2</u>
<u>6. Negative prefixes 3</u>
<u>7. Negative prefixes 4</u>

English has a variety of negative prefixes, some of which came into English from Latin or French, and some of which came directly from Old English. This variety means that in some cases a word can take two different prefixes with two different meanings. In other cases, two synonyms may take different negative prefixes with the same meanings.

In certain cases a basic form will take one prefix, and a derivation from that form will take a different prefix. Some prefixes have different forms depending on the pronunciation of the first letter in the word that they prefix, e.g.: *in+legal - illegal, in+possible - impossible*. Students should read the instructions for each exercise for more information.

<u>8. Suffixes 1</u>
<u>9. Suffixes 2</u>
<u>10. Suffixes 3</u>

Suffixes are added to words to create new words, which are usually, but not always, different parts of speech. For example, the suffix *-ation* creates nouns from verbs: *centralise → centralisation*. These exercises practise situations when two suffixes can form words with different meanings from the same root, e.g. *apply → appliance, application*.

These exercises practise groups of words which are linked by a theme. The theme is given for each exercise. These exercises make it easier for students to remember new words by associating them with other words in the same category.

Collocations are combinations of two or more words which tend to go together in language use. Although in most cases they are not governed by grammar rules, they are important for students precisely because they show how the language is actually used in real communication.

Take, for example, the noun *handshake*. We can use different adjectives with it, but certain adjectives tend to be used more often than others: *firm handshake, limp handshake*. Often a collocation can look strange on the surface, but has a special, colloquial meaning: *golden handshake* - "money paid to someone when they leave a job". Although we can say *golden handshake*, we never say *silver handshake*.

These exercises help students to raise their awareness of collocations and practise some of the more common ones. Students should make it a habit to notice and learn collocations. In this way they will develop a very good feeling for natural language use in English and vastly increase their vocabulary base.

1. Words with or without a-: adjective - adverb

Each of these adjectives creates a predicative adjective or an adverb with the prefix a-. Put the appropriate form of each one, with or without a-, in the correct space.

back, broad, like, live, loud, lone, wry

1. On the flight over I was the _____ passenger in first class. It was fantastic having nobody else around.
2. I really hate _____ people. They think everyone needs to hear them.
3. Most snakes lay eggs, but some give birth to _____ young.
4. As I watched the train pull out of the deserted station, I looked around and then the realisation hit me: I was finally completely _____.
5. Can you take this book _____ to the library for me if you're going there?
6. I can't believe James and Ryan aren't brothers. I mean, they look so _____ that it's difficult to tell which one is which.
7. Pete always manages to come out with a _____ comment when he sees someone famous making a fool of themselves. He's so witty.
8. Tony's so much _____ his father. He takes after him a lot. He even has the same mannerisms and talks in the same way.
9. When you travel to many places, you have to have a _____ mind or you might constantly be offended by local customs and practices.
10. I was completely taken _____ by the news that my brother had been arrested for armed robbery. It was a total surprise.
11. Some people find it's easier to learn new vocabulary if they read it _____ so that they can hear the pronunciation.
12. I'll have to keep a close watch on the preparations for the wedding to make sure things don't go _____. It would be terrible if anything went wrong.
13. I'm fed up with living in this country. The weather's so bad and it's so expensive. I'm going to move _____, somewhere hot like Australia.
14. It's an incredible story of survival. Tim Hicks was lost for ten days in the desert with little food and water, but searchers still found him _____.

2. Words with or without *a*-: noun - adverb

Each of these nouns creates an adverb with the prefix *a*-. Put the appropriate form of each one, with or without *a*-, in the correct space.

breast, head, loft, pace, shore, side

1. It's taken weeks for the research project to start up. It was slow at first but now it's gathered _____ and we'll definitely finish it on time.

2. We've got too much stuff that we don't use taking up space in the bedroom. Let's put it out of the way, up in the _____.

3. The sea crossing was so rough that I got really seasick, but once we were safely _____ in France, I felt much better.

4. Some people say that the _____ of the chicken is the tastiest part, but I prefer the wing.

5. The _____ of government in this country is the Prime Minister, since we don't have a president in our system.

6. We walked along the _____ looking for seashells to take home and decorate the house.

7. My main job was working in an office, but in the evenings I worked as a taxi driver on the _____ for extra money.

8. If we keep walking for bit longer, we'll come to a nice country pub not far _____, where we can have our lunch and a nice drink.

9. The plane accelerated along the runway for what seemed like ages, but soon we were _____ and flying over the houses far below.

10. After the class, I took Maria _____ from the other students and told her that she wouldn't be able to take the exam. She was very upset.

11. The building of the new stadium is continuing _____ and it should be completed on schedule in two months.

12. At one point the gorge becomes so narrow that no more than two people walking _____ can go through it.

3. Words with or without *a-*: verb - adjective/adverb

Each of these verbs creates a predicative adjective or an adverb with the prefix *a-*.
Put the appropriate form of each one, with or without *a-*, in the correct space.

board, drift, float, part, skew, sleep, wake

1. John and Jason are the ultimate twins. They do everything together and it's impossible to _____ them, even for an hour.
2. I need to _____ up really early in the morning. I've got to catch the early plane to New York at 8.00.
3. Can you keep the noise down? The children are _____.
4. Last night in the storm my boat broke free from its mooring and started to _____ out to sea. It's a long way out now.
5. You have to be careful when you conduct this experiment. If you leave it too long it can _____ the results, making them too high.
6. I was so worried about the exam today that I couldn't sleep. I lay _____ all night thinking about it.
7. I really enjoyed that balloon ride. It was fantastic to _____ through the air over the fields and houses.
8. Good morning everyone. This is your captain speaking. I'd like to welcome you _____ and I hope you enjoy your cruise around the islands.
9. Kate and Harry love each other so much that they hate to be _____ for more than a day. They just have to be together.
10. As a result of the mutiny on the ship, the captain and his officers were put in one of the lifeboats and cast _____ on the open sea.
11. After the cruise ship hit the iceberg, it stayed _____ for less than an hour before it started to sink.
12. Everything was fine until it started to rain. Now my plans for a day out are all _____. We'll have to plan something else to do.
13. I'm really tired. I'm going to _____ now. See you in the morning.
14. There's no rush. We don't have to _____ the plane for another hour.

4. Negative prefixes 1

The words in the right box need to be negative. Choose a negative prefix from the left box, attach it to the appropriate word and put it in the appropriate sentence. Each prefix is used twice. Remember that *non-* keeps the hyphen.

anti-, de-, dis-, non-, in/im/il/ir-, un-	acceptable, approve, clockwise, compose, considerate, desirable, event, flexible, order, septic, stabilise, stop

1. Honestly! Joanne's so _____. She just does what she likes and doesn't care how it affects other people.

2. I scratched my arm but don't worry, it's not bleeding. I'll just put some _____ on it and it'll be fine.

3. I went the open-air concert yesterday, but it rained all day and only one band played. Most people were disappointed. It was a bit of a _____.

4. There are fears that the demonstrations and riots in the streets of the capital could _____ the government and possibly bring it down.

5. I thought that the amount of compensation that the travel company offered me for my holiday disaster was completely _____, so I refused it.

6. When Mike took over as managing director, the company was in total _____, but he's really sorted things out and we're doing really well.

7. I'm so tired I'm going straight to bed. I've driven _____ all the way from London. That's over 200 miles.

8. The mummy's tomb was so well sealed that the body did not _____ very much and was well preserved.

9. There's a high fence all round the property to keep _____ people out.

10. You drive almost halfway round the ring-road in an _____ direction and then take exit 25. That will take you straight into the city centre.

11. Ken just won't change his mind under any circumstances, no matter whether he's right or wrong. He's so _____.

12. I want to be a singer, but my parents _____. They say it's not a real career, like teaching or medicine.

5. Negative prefixes 2

The words in the right box need to be negative. Choose a negative prefix from the left box, attach it to the appropriate word and put it in the appropriate sentence. Each prefix is used twice. Remember that *non-* and *no-* keep the hyphen.

anti-, de-, dis-, no-, in/im/il/ir-, non-, un-	attractive, climax, go, honest, hoper, hurt, personal, qualified, regulate, responsible, stick, value, violent, virus

1. Mahatma Ghandi believed that India had to gain independence through _____ means and not through fighting and killing.

2. The problem with doing business in this country is all the rules and bureaucracy. The government needs to _____ it.

3. The atmosphere in the stadium was electric and we all expected a great game, but both teams played really badly. It was a real _____.

4. Don't believe anything Jenny says. She's a really _____ person.

5. You should never leave a dog locked in a car in hot weather. It's a very _____ thing to do as they could easily overheat and die.

6. My brother was involved in a serious accident last night. Luckily, he escaped _____, but it was quite a shock for him.

7. Why is Jim taking the exam? He won't pass it. He's a real _____.

8. Make sure your computer has _____ software on it or you could well get infected through an email or programme.

9. Some parts of the city are dangerous _____ areas. They are too violent for most people to visit.

10. The police arrested Ron for driving while _____. He had lost his licence the month before for speeding.

11. If your neighbourhood is dirty and untidy it could _____ your property when you want to sell it.

12. Mary thinks she's _____, but I think she's really pretty.

13. This frying pan's _____, so it's very easy to wash after cooking.

14. I don't like the new manager. I find him rather cold and _____. I can't imagine being friendly with him.

6. Negative prefixes 3

The words in the right box need to be negative. However, different prefixes are used with words from the same root and words with very similar meanings. Choose a negative prefix from the left box, attach it to the appropriate word from each pair and put them in the appropriate sentences.

dis-, in/im/il/ir-, un-	balance, balanced; believable, credible; comfort, comfortable; equal, equality; just, justice; likely, probable; secure, sure; stability, stable

1. Harriet has to build up her self-confidence. She's very _____ of herself and needs to be less _____. She's capable of a lot more.

2. I can't stand flying economy class on long distance flights. It's so _____. There's less _____ in first class.

3. I find it _____ that Gordon failed his driving test for the tenth time. It's absolutely _____ that he simply can't get it right.

4. It's completely unacceptable in this day and age that women's pay should be _____ to men's. We need to end this kind of _____ now and raise women's pay to the same level as men's.

5. Of course, it's possible that humans will walk on Mars by 2010, but rather _____. I think it's _____ to happen before 2020.

6. Because the ground dried out so much in the summer, it led to serious _____ in the foundations of our house, so we had to move out when the house started to become too _____ to stay in.

7. I think it's _____ that victims of crime have to wait so long for their cases to come to court. We must put a stop to this _____.

8. The doctor told me that my body chemistry is _____, which is why I keep getting sick. I have to take these drugs to correct the _____.

7. Negative prefixes 4

Some words have two different negative forms. Choose either *dis-* or *un-* from the left box, attach it to the appropriate word and put it in the appropriate sentence. Each word is used twice, once with each prefix.

dis-, un-	able, affected, connected, cover, interested, used

1. I'm fed up with teaching. I've been doing it far too long. I'm going to find another job completely _____ with it, like advertising or sales.

2. Banks only recommend their own financial products. You should talk to someone completely _____, like an independent financial adviser.

3. My brother's a property developer. He looks for old, _____ schools and churches to buy up and convert into luxury flats.

4. When you've been helping students with their studies all year, it's difficult to tell them that you're _____ to help them in their exam.

5. Police today arrested ten people in London following a two-year operation to _____ a plot to flood the country with counterfeit money.

6. We had an earthquake in our town last week. It was scary, but luckily for us, our house was relatively _____, just a few broken roof tiles.

7. For sale: brand new laptop computer, still in box, completely _____. Unwanted gift. Only £500, or near offer.

8. Hackers managed to _____ the firewall on the local bank's computer system and gain access to customer passwords and IDs.

9. Scientists say that in the future, overpopulation will force people to leave Earth and travel across the galaxy to _____ new planets to colonise.

10. If we don't pay the electricity bill, the company will _____ us from the mains supply and we'll have to pay a lot to get back on again.

11. After the poor reviews of his first film, Jim Layne was so _____ and disheartened that he didn't make another one for five years.

12. I told Jane that her best friend was on the phone, but she looked completely _____ and just carried on watching TV.

8. Suffixes 1

These word pairs are from the same root word but with different suffixes and meanings. Choose the correct word for each gap.

apparition, appearance; appliance, application; considerable, considerate;
momentary, momentous; popular, populous; residence, residency

1. Over the last week we have given _____ thought to your offer of $10m for our business, but we are afraid that it's too low as it stands.

2. So finally, after seven years of planning, the 2012 London Olympic Games are declared open. This is a truly _____ occasion!

3. I opened the door slowly and looked into the dark house. It was then that I saw a ghostly _____, but it was gone in an instant.

4. The President's official _____ is the White House, though he also owns three private houses of his own.

5. Have you sent in your _____ for that job? I'm sure you'll get it. You've got the right qualifications and plenty of experience.

6. China is the most _____ country in the world, with over 1.3 billion people.

7. Charles had a _____ lapse of concentration on the motorway, but it resulted in a fatal car accident that will live with him forever.

8. Although the crowd waited over an hour for Madonna to come on stage for the concert, they went wild when she finally made her _____.

9. In the latest opinion polls, only 21% of the voting public support Terry Bloor. He's the least _____ prime minister in history.

10. If foreign nationals want to get _____ in this country, they need to show that they have a job and plenty of money.

11. Before you buy any electrical _____, like a fridge or cooker, these days, check that it uses as little electricity as possible.

12. Thank you for all your help and support for my university application. You've been so kind and _____.

9. Suffixes 2

These word pairs are from the same root word but with different suffixes and meanings. Choose the correct word for each gap.

expectancy, expectation; expenditure, expense; governance, government; publication. publicity; reality, realism; reasonable, reasoned

1. We need to be far more careful with money. Over the last year the company's _____ has increased by over 30%, but our income hasn't risen.

2. The editor has discovered some factual errors in your new book, so we have delayed its _____ for a month in order to correct them.

3. The country needs an election and a new _____, and our party is the best choice. The sooner we have an election, the better.

4. Our _____ was that most students would pass the exam, but in the event it was so hard that only half of them managed to pass.

5. Henry put forward such an intelligent and _____ argument in the debate that no one could disagree with him.

6. It's fine to have an overall political philosophy, but you have to combine it with a degree of _____ if you want to hold power.

7. Over the last century, average life _____ in this country has increased by over twenty years and now stands at around 74.

8. The problem with this organisation is one of _____. There is no one at the top who is really taking it in the right direction.

9. Nowadays a music group can get huge _____ simply by setting up a website and uploading videos of their performances for fans to download.

10. After the damage to the computer system when it crashed, we had to set everything up again at massive _____.

11. Many people have the mistaken idea that teaching is an easy job. The _____ is that it is one of the most demanding jobs anyone can do.

12. The manager is a very _____ person. I'm sure she'll be happy to listen to your ideas and take them up if they're good.

10. Suffixes 3

These word pairs are from the same root word but with different suffixes and meanings. Choose the correct word for each gap.

exposition, exposure; honourable, honorary; installation, instalment; instance, instant; locality, location; pronouncement, pronunciation

1. The next property that we're going to see is in a wonderful _____ next to a lake, with beautiful views of the surrounding hills and woods.

2. In his latest _____ on the future of education, the Prime Minister outlined new policies to improve exam results and create more university places.

3. In view of John's wonderful work for us over the years, we have made him _____ life president of our society. Congratulations, John.

4. A big lottery win can transform your life in an _____.

5. I'm going to Paris on Friday for the new _____ of modern design. It's the biggest event of the year. People are coming from all over the world.

6. If you choose to pay monthly for the computer, you'll need to pay a first _____ of £69, followed by eleven more of £50.

7. This is the first _____ of bad behaviour from this class, so they won't be punished severely this time. They're usually very well-behaved.

8. The problem for anyone romantically involved with a prince these days is the media _____ that goes along with it. You have no privacy at all.

9. This is exactly the sort of _____ which people want to live in. It's a very well-off, middle class area, with good transport connections and schools.

10. Your reading and writing are very good, but you need to improve your speaking, especially your _____.

11. In a very rare but _____ act, the company's managers have given up their bonuses to keep the money in the company and save workers' jobs.

12. I'm still waiting for the gas fitter to come round and complete the _____ of my new gas cooker. I can't do it myself.

11. Categories 1 - Abstractions 1

Each of the words in the box denotes an abstraction. Choose the most appropriate one for each sentence. Use the plural if necessary.

behaviour, concept, conflict, custom, emotion, skill, ideology, offence, penalty, sense, vice, virtue

1. Many people enter politics with a particular _____, like capitalism or socialism, but the reality of modern politics often changes them.

2. If you want to be a nurse you need to display a number of _____, such as patience, perseverance and understanding.

3. The government intends to increase prison sentences for a number of serious _____, such as physical assault and drink-driving.

4. There are still many old English _____ which are practised in the countryside, like cheese rolling and Morris dancing.

5. When I saw the exam results I had mixed _____ – elation for myself, but disappointment for my best friend, who failed her exams.

6. Of the five _____ that we have, the two we tend to use most are our sight and hearing.

7. I can't understand my boyfriend's _____. One minute it's all love and affection, the next minute he hardly wants to know me.

8. Many of the _____ we take for granted today, such as democracy and freedom, come from ancient Greek thought and culture.

9. Before you go to university you need to improve your study _____, like researching, note-taking and summarising.

10. People have to learn to deal with their _____, like greed and envy, and control them if they are to live happier lives.

11. The _____ for theft range from a fine, through community service, to imprisonment.

12. Couples have to learn to deal with _____ in their lives, like disagreements, arguments and quarrels.

12. Categories 2 - Abstractions 2

Each of the words in the box denotes an abstraction. Choose the most appropriate one for each sentence. Use the plural if necessary.

celebration, disaster, discovery, entertainment, event, function, institution, invention, phenomenon, shelter, technology, treatment

1. If you like _____ this town has plenty of it - nightclubs, cinemas, theatres and concerts.

2. Penicillin and aspirin were two of the great medical _____ of the twentieth century.

3. Scientists are developing new ways of predicting natural _____, like earthquakes and hurricanes.

4. Nowadays there are a number of different _____ for cancer, including radiotherapy and chemotherapy.

5. This army knife has a number of _____. You can use it as a screwdriver, a tin opener or a nail file.

6. It's getting dark. We need to find some _____ for the night. There should be a hut about a kilometre ahead.

7. The government has announced plans to reform some of the major national _____, including the army and the police.

8. People often mistake natural _____, like lightning and meteors, for unidentified flying objects and alien spaceships.

9. Some of the greatest _____ in history, like the television and computer, were never expected to catch on as much as they have.

10. I think it's really important for the family to come together for big _____, like birthdays and anniversaries.

11. We hold various _____ in this hall. Last month we had a classical concert, a book fair and an art exhibition.

12. I love new _____, especially digital cameras and camcorders. I always like to buy the latest products.

13. Categories 3 - Food

Each of the words in the box refers to food. Choose the most appropriate one for each sentence. Use the plural if necessary.

beverage, cereal, condiment, dairy, delicacy, herb, poultry, produce, pulses, seafood, spice, spirits

1. Indian cooking is famous for its use of _____, especially turmeric, nutmeg and saffron.

2. The government has advised _____ farmers to lock up their hens and turkeys to prevent the spread of bird flu.

3. We have various hot _____ on sale, like tea and coffee.

4. The only _____ I really like is cornflakes. I don't like anything made from rice or wheat.

5. Would you like to try any of our _____? We have caviar, frog's legs and quail's eggs. They're of the best quality.

6. People are buying more _____ products these days, especially butter, yoghurt and cottage cheese.

7. You can find the mustard and brown sauce on the _____ shelves in aisle 14 of the supermarket.

8. Always carefully check the _____ in a market before you buy it, to make sure it's fresh, in particular strawberries, grapes and leaf vegetables.

9. We've got enough wine and beer for the party, but we need some more _____. Can you go out and get some whisky and vodka?

10. This town is famous for its _____. All the shrimps and squid are freshly caught every day.

11. Nutritionists recommend _____, like lentils and beans, as an important source of protein and carbohydrates.

12. I love cooking with lots of Mediterranean _____, like basil and thyme, though they have to be fresh.

14. Categories 4 - Objects

Each of the words in the box relates to types of object. Choose the most appropriate one for each sentence. Use the plural if necessary.

appliance, equipment, gadget, hardware, instrument, material, ornament, stationery, tool, utensil, vehicle, weapon

1. Can you play a musical _____? We need someone who can play the guitar and piano for our new rock group.

2. I've checked all the climbing _____ for our Alpine expedition. We've got enough rope, but we need another pick and a hammer.

3. They've got some lovely _____ in this gift shop. I particularly like the vases and little figurines that they sell.

4. Electrical stores often try to sell _____ with extended warranties, though most cookers and fridges don't need them.

5. I'm not sure what _____ this shirt's made of. It looks like silk and feels like satin, but it's as cheap as cotton.

6. John's always buying _____ that he doesn't need. He's just got an electric toothbrush, an MP3 player and a car key detector.

7. Can you order some new _____ from our supplier? We need pens, paper and plastic folders.

8. When the police searched the murder suspect's car, they found various _____, including three knives and a gun.

9. All my computer _____ is new, except for the printer, which I had with my last computer.

10. No motor _____ are allowed in this road except for residents' cars and motorbikes.

11. Can you get me a hammer and a screwdriver from my bag of _____ over there?

12. There aren't enough cooking _____ in the kitchen. There isn't even a pan or spatula for frying eggs.

15. Categories 5 - Animals

Each of the words in the box refers to animals. Choose the most appropriate one for each sentence. Use the plural if necessary.

amphibian, fauna, insect, livestock, mammal, mollusc, predator, primate, reptile, shellfish, vermin, wildfowl

1. The aquarium is running an exhibition of octopuses, squids and other types of

   _____.

2. There's a country park here where you can see a lot of _____,

   such as ducks, geese and pheasants.

3. A new nature reserve is going to be created to protect endangered species of

   _____, in particular gorillas and chimpanzees.

4. A lot of _____, like mussels and oysters, are edible.

5. Farmers have been advised to check all their _____, in particular

   sheep and cows, for foot and mouth disease.

6. All _____ start life in water, though some frogs and toads live their

   adult lives mostly on land.

7. The _____ of the Galapagos Islands, including the tortoises,

   iguanas and birds, is found nowhere else in the world.

8. The chief _____ on the African plains are big cats, like lions,

   leopards and cheetahs.

9. People have always tried to get rid of _____ which live in their

   houses, especially rats and cockroaches.

10. All _____, from apes to elephants and kangaroos, feed their

    young with milk.

11. Australia has a huge variety of _____, especially poisonous

    snakes, giant lizards and huge crocodiles.

12. All _____ go through a larval stage, though the most fascinating

    and colourful are the caterpillars of butterflies and moths.

16. Collocations 1 - Adjective + Noun

Choose an adjective from the box on the left and a noun from the box on the right and put them together in the appropriate sentence.

awkward, expert, false, first-hand, heated, lukewarm, nasty, puzzled, typical, vivid	account, claim, discussion, feature, imagination, look, moment, opinion, response, shock

1. After his release, the hostage gave the press a _____ _____ of his treatment by the armed group which had held him.

2. A lot of holidaymakers make a _____ _____ for compensation on their travel insurance when they haven't actually lost anything.

3. During the staff meeting there was a _____ _____ about our financial problems, which led to some staff walking out in anger.

4. A _____ _____ of modern city life is the congestion caused by the huge volume of traffic that goes in and out every day.

5. Jimmy's got a really _____ _____. Yesterday he told me that saw an alien in a field. It turned out to be a scarecrow.

6. As I was driving through Spain, I stopped to ask for directions, but the man just gave me a _____ _____. I realised that he couldn't understand a word I was saying.

7. While my new wife and I were waiting for our meal in the restaurant, a woman at the next table turned round and I suddenly realised it was my ex-wife. I just smiled and said hello, but it was a very _____ _____.

8. This is such an important financial decision that I think we have to get an _____ _____ before we decide what to do.

9. Do you remember Jim from our class at school? I emailed him the other day, but he gave me a very _____ _____. I don't think he was very keen to meet me again for some reason.

10. When we got home in the evening, we had a very _____ _____. The front door was open and the house had been burgled.

17. Collocations 2 - Noun + Verb

Choose a noun from the box on the left and a verb from the box on the right and put them together in the appropriate sentence and in the appropriate forms.

crime, doubt, heart, jaw, mind, patience, reputation, rumour, smile, sunlight	arise, circulate, drop, freeze, grow, leap, pay, pour, snap, wander

1. People don't believe that _____ _____, but in reality many criminals get away with it and are never caught.

2. Watson told the police that he had been at a restaurant at the time of the murder, but _____ _____ when none of the restaurant staff could remember him being there.

3. I thought my son had gone missing but when I picked up the phone and heard his voice, my _____ _____. He was safe and sound!

4. When John saw my new sports car his _____ _____. He couldn't believe I had actually bought one. He was so envious!

5. When I'm on the train in the morning, I like to let my _____ _____. It passes the time nicely thinking about all kinds of things.

6. I asked the waiter three times why our food was taking so long. After an hour of waiting my _____ _____ and we walked out.

7. Johnson's playing so well that his _____ _____. Soon a big football club will notice him and pay a lot of money for him.

8. So many _____ _____ about the Prime Minister's future that he had to state publicly that he had no intention of resigning.

9. Simon confidently laid his cards out on the table, but the _____ _____ on his face when he saw my cards had beaten his.

10. I got up, stretched and opened the curtains. Bright _____ _____ into the room at the start of a beautiful day.

18. Collocations 3 - Verb + Noun

Choose a verb from the box on the left and a noun from the box on the right and put them together in the appropriate sentence and in the appropriate forms.

cause, change, cheat, crack, drag, erase, learn, shed, show, swap	course, death, feet, joke, lesson, light, past, places, promise, scene

1. Criticism of the government's policies increased today, but the Prime Minister insisted that it would continue to pursue them and not _____ _____. He said there was no other alternative to them.

2. In the past people believed that there existed a fountain of youth that could help them _____ _____ and live forever.

3. I tried to get the management to make a quick decision on the proposed company merger, but they're really _____ their _____.

4. John's a great person to have on a long trip. He really makes people laugh, _____ _____ all the time.

5. I hope you've _____ your _____. Don't ever take the car again without asking me. You're lucky the police didn't arrest you.

6. Officials don't know how the plane crash happened, but they are hoping that this new enquiry is going to _____ some _____ on it.

7. The police found out that after Malone left prison, he tried to _____ his _____ and start a new life of crime in another country.

8. If you really think that going out to work is far harder than staying at home and taking care of the kids, let's _____ _____ for a week and see if you can cope.

9. Amy's _____ _____ in her tennis, though she needs to pay more attention to her backhand. I'm sure she'll be a top player if she practises.

10. Look. I know you don't like my mother, but we're going out to have dinner together and I don't want you to _____ a _____ at the restaurant in front of everyone.

19. Collocations 4 - Noun + Noun

Choose a noun from the box on the left and a noun from the box on the right and put them together in the appropriate sentence.

culture, generation, killer, market, media, parrot, safety, sex, style, trial	fashion, gap, guru, image, instinct, net, period, shock, symbol, value

1. When I first arrived in Japan it was a massive _____ _____ for me, but I soon got used to living there.

2. It's one thing to learn something and really understand it, and another thing entirely to learn to repeat it _____ _____ without understanding its meaning.

3. I know Tim's a teenager, but he gets on with his grandfather really well. There's just no _____ _____ between them.

4. Ricardo is currently the best football striker in the world. He has a real _____ _____ in front of goal and rarely misses.

5. I got a really good price for my house when I sold it, about £10,000 above the _____ _____ for this type of property.

6. If you want to be president you have to develop a really good _____ _____ on TV and in the press, as that's how voters will judge you.

7. We're going to take you on for a _____ _____ of three months at our head office, and if you do well, you'll have a permanent job.

8. Antonio is the biggest _____ _____ in the fashion business. People always love his designs and creations and listen to what he says.

9. Marilyn Munroe was probably the most famous _____ _____ of the 1950s and 1960s. Men really loved her.

10. The social security system was originally set up as a _____ _____ for people who couldn't work and had no other source of income, but it's being abused more and more dishonest people.

20. Collocations 5 - Quantifier + Noun

Choose a quantifier from the box on the left and a noun from the box on the right and put them together in the appropriate sentence.

couple, dash, grain, host, level, member, pile, plume, series, volume	*colour, junk, interest, meetings, minutes, sales, smoke, staff, stars, truth*

1. The decoration in this room's quite boring, so I've got some flowers to add a

    _____ of _____ to it.

2. Don't tell me that you paid £1000 for that _____ of

    _____! You must be crazy! That car's not even worth £100, it's so

    old!

3. Can you wait down here for a _____ of _____ while I

    finish getting myself ready?

4. You know that story about the dog trapped in the hole in the ground? It

    generated a high _____ of _____ in the papers.

5. The management and union representatives are holding a _____

    of _____ to try to settle the strike and get back to work.

6. Ever since we introduced our new broadband mobile phone onto the market in

    June, the _____ of _____ has doubled every month.

7. As we approached the house we could see a long _____ of

    _____ rising into the sky. The house was on fire!

8. I'm sorry, but I don't work here. You need to speak to a _____ of

    _____. There's one over there at the desk.

9. I went to a charity event last night to raise money for children's charities. There

    was a _____ of _____ there, including Tom Cruise

    and Michael Jackson.

10. I know Barry tends to make things up and exaggerate a lot of the time, but

    there's a _____ of _____ in what he said about the

    music industry.

WORD FOCUS

This section consists of twenty exercises dealing with single common words which have a variety of meanings, collocations, expressions and associations. Some of them are literal and some are abstract or metaphorical.

In some cases one or more words have to be changed to fit grammatically into the sentence. These are usually tense changes for verbs and sometimes plurals for nouns. Each exercise has instructions for the completion of that particular exercise.

Contents

1. Change

Choose the correct word or phrase to go in the gaps in the sentences. You may have to change some forms to fit the sentences.

changeable, change down, change hands, change over, change round, for a change, loose change, no change, sea change, small change

1. During the civil war the town _____ three times, until it was finally captured and held by the Southern Army.
2. If you see traffic lights ahead, be ready to _____ through the gears so that, if the lights go red, you can stop smoothly in a low gear.
3. I try not to carry a lot of _____ around in my pockets, just enough to buy a drink or a snack if I need it.
4. Ever since Maurice had his accident, there's been a _____ in his behaviour. Before it, he was confident and sociable, but now he's moody and unfriendly.
5. The doctors say that there's _____ in Dad's condition. He's still critical, but we hope he will improve.
6. The weather is so _____ these days that you don't know what clothes to put on when you go out or whether to take an umbrella.
7. Stanley's so rich that a £50 note is just _____ to him, just like three or four pounds would be to us.
8. Can you help me move this sofa to the other wall? I like to _____ the furniture in here every few months to keep the house looking fresh.
9. I'm fed up with staying in and watching TV. Let's do something different tonight. We can go out to a club and spend a bit of money _____.
10. We're still using the old computer system, but we're going to _____ to the new one after the summer holiday.

2. End 1

Choose the correct word or phrase to go in the gaps in the sentences. You don't need to change any forms to fit the sentences.

a sticky end, at an end, at the deep end, at the end, ending, in the end, on the receiving end, no end, on end, split ends

1. That was a great trick you played on Joe. He's tricked me so many times that it's great to see him _____ for a change.
2. We spent a week thinking about where to go for our summer holiday, but _____ we decided to go camping in France.
3. I won't tell you the _____ of the film because that'll spoil it. It's really worth seeing. You have to go.
4. I believe that if you want to succeed in anything you should jump in _____. Don't waste time trying to learn gradually.
5. I need to go to the hairdresser's. I've got so many _____ in my hair that it's really untidy and I can't comb it.
6. Don't worry. All the exam results are coming out tomorrow morning, so your waiting will be _____.
7. Bonny and Clyde were famous bank robbers in America in the 1930s, but they came to _____ when armed police killed them in an ambush on their car.
8. This is the best book I've ever read. The plot twists and turns all the way through, and _____ there's an unexpected shock.
9. You won't be able to get the sofa into the lounge the normal way. You have to stand it up _____ to get it round the door.
10. At the beginning of the football season there was _____ of people saying that our team would go down, but we've proved them all wrong. What a fantastic season!

3. End 2

Choose the correct word or phrase to go in the gaps in the sentences. You may have to change some forms to fit the sentences.

at my wits' end, end in, end it all, end up, end with, make ends meet, put an end to, the bitter end, the end of the world, to end

1. Jane and Terry have split up. She should have listened to me when I said he was wrong for her and it would all _____ tears.

2. The Standing Stones' concert was really great. They played all their old hits and some recent ones, and _____ their latest song.

3. The thing about running a marathon is that no matter how hard it gets, you can't give up. You must keep on to _____.

4. I've decided to talk to the press and tell them the truth about my private life to _____ all this gossip and speculation.

5. Life had become so difficult for Tina that she took fifty sleeping pills to try to _____. Luckily, we found her and she's recovering in hospital.

6. We tried to find the ferry port, but the signposting on the motorway was so bad that we got completely lost and _____ missing the ferry.

7. With the hurricane on its way, people are panic buying in the shops and boarding up their houses, like it's _____.

8. My salary just about covers the rent, food and travel, but it's really difficult to _____, so my wife is going to get a job.

9. My daughter came in after midnight last night, even though I told her to be back at 10.00. I was _____ with worry.

10. And now, _____, I'd like to thank you all for coming here today and making this event such a success. Goodbye, and have a safe journey home.

4. Fall 1

Choose the correct word or phrase to go in the gaps in the sentences. You may have to change some forms to fit the sentences.

falls, fallout, downfall, rainfall, freefall, fall guy, windfall, crestfallen, falloff, pitfall

1. I've just had a real _____. Last year I bought 100 shares in a company for £1000, and I've just sold them for £10,000! Isn't that fantastic?

2. Although the Finance Minister was forced to resign because of the illegal loans scandal, the _____ could also affect the Prime Minister, who apparently knew about it but covered it up.

3. At 1000 metres, Angel _____ on the Roraima Plateau in Venezuela are the highest in the world. Some of the water doesn't even reach the bottom, but gets blown away in the wind.

4. While all the other students celebrated their exam passes, Henry just sat alone _____. He had failed all his exams after expecting good results.

5. It's a great idea to start a new company, but there are a lot of _____ which can lead to failure, like not getting paid by customers, or borrowing too much money from the bank that you can't pay back.

6. Although Toby was convicted, he was just the _____. The gang let him take the blame and go to prison for the robbery, while they got away.

7. Before the election the president's popularity stood at 65%, but since the tax rises it's gone into _____, down to only 20%, and it's still dropping fast.

8. Garden stores report that there's been a slight _____ in the sales of barbecues owing to the wet weather, but they should pick up again soon when the good weather comes back.

9. This month's _____ has been 2cm, double the usual for this time of year, and has led to flooding in some areas of the country.

10. It wasn't the last prime minister's numerous love affairs that led to his eventual _____, but the lies he told about them to the public.

5. Fall 2

Choose the correct verb phrase to go in the gaps in the sentences. You may have to change some forms and tenses to fit the sentences.

fall about, fall apart, fall away, fall down, fall for, fall in, fall into, fall on, fall out, fall over, fall to, fall under

1. I don't trust those boys and I don't want Jimmy playing with them in case he _____ bad habits, like drinking and staying out late.
2. Honestly! You really should go and see that film. It was so funny we just _____ laughing from beginning to end.
3. After my father died we _____ hard times. We had to leave the house and go and live in a one-room flat on benefits. It was really hard to cope.
4. As soon as Diana walked in the room, I knew she was the one for me. She was so beautiful that I _____ her straight away. It was love at first sight.
5. When Harry told me he was really sorry for the awful things that he had done to me, all the anger and hurt I felt just _____. I gave him a big hug.
6. Jenny's marriage _____ when she discovered that her husband had been sleeping with her sister. She felt she could never forgive him.
7. After our night out clubbing, all my friends were drunk, so it _____ me to drive home as I was the only one who hadn't drunk anything.
8. When Colin met Celia, he completely _____ her spell. He's madly in love and he'll do anything for her, but she's just using him for his money.
9. The employers claim that pay rises damage jobs, but if you compare their argument with the facts it completely _____.
10. Jan and Joy were best friends until Jack came along. They _____ over which one was his girlfriend and now they haven't talked for weeks
11. It snowed so hard last night that part of our house roof _____ under the weight. Luckily, we were out at the time, but there's a lot of damage.
12. My grandmother had to go to hospital last night because she _____ in the kitchen and broke her hip.

6. Fall 3

Choose the correct word or phrase to go in the gaps in the sentences. You may have to change some forms to fit the sentences.

fall back on, fall foul, fall from grace, fall ill, fall into a trap, fall into place, fall in with, fall over oneself, fall through, fall to pieces

1. After Tony's wife walked out on him, his life just _____. He lost his job and his house and started drinking. Poor guy! Now he sleeps in the streets.

2. Katie was studying really well, but then she _____ the wrong people, started taking drugs and dropped out of university.

3. You should get travel insurance in case you _____ abroad or have an accident and have to be brought back home. It can cost a lot of money.

4. Our plans for a great day out completely _____. The coach came an hour late and broke down on the way to the seaside, and then it started raining. In the end, we just came home early.

5. Remember. When you sell your house, you have to decide on the lowest offer that you will accept from the buyers. Don't _____ and accept the first offer that they make, or you'll regret it. You can always get more.

6. As soon as Michael Jackson appeared, the crowd rushed forward and people were _____ to meet him and shake his hand.

7. Very few people have _____ of the new law banning smoking in public places. Most seem to be obeying it.

8. One minute Ricardo was the most popular and respected football player in the world, but then he _____ because of that one act of violence on the field.

9. I'm taking enough money to last for the whole trip, but if anything happens, I've got a few hundred pounds in the bank to _____ if I need it.

10. When I started my driving lessons, I found it really difficult to use the clutch and change gear, but about a week before my driving test it all _____ and I passed easily first time.

7. Fit

Choose the correct phrase to go in the gaps in the sentences. You may have to change some forms to fit the sentences.

fit for, fit in, fit out, fitting, fit to, fit up, good fit, have a fit, in fits, keep-fit, outfit, see fit

1. I get out of breath just running for the bus these days. I need to do more exercise, so I'm going to join a _____ class at my local leisure centre.

2. Before you go climbing, we have to _____ you _____ with the right clothes and equipment, like ropes, helmet and boots.

3. Do you like my new _____? I bought it in that new fashion shop in the high street. They sell really good clothes at low prices.

4. Government health inspectors have prosecuted three butcher's shops for selling meat that was not _____ human consumption.

5. Good morning everyone, and welcome back to school. I'd like to welcome the new students and hope you will all help them to _____.

6. You really have to go and see this film. It's so funny. I was _____ all through it. I just couldn't stop laughing.

7. These shoes are nice and comfortable and a really _____. Also, I like the style. I'll take them.

8. You've been drinking too much. You're not _____ drive, so give me the keys to the car and I'll run you home.

9. I'm really angry with John. He _____ to let people stay in my house while I was away, and they left the place in a complete mess.

10. It's my parents' fiftieth wedding anniversary on Saturday, so we're having a big party. I'm writing a _____ speech for it.

11. The new house has a really nice, big kitchen, but we'll have to _____ it _____ completely with new appliances before we move in.

12. My mum will _____ when she sees the broken window, and it's not a good idea to be around when she loses her temper, believe me!

8. Hand 1

Choose the correct phrase to go in the gaps in the sentences. You may have to change some forms to fit the sentences.

at hand, at one's own hands, by hand, hand in glove, hand in hand, in hand, in one's hands, off one's hands, on hand, on one's hands, out of hand, to hand

1. The president is a dictator with blood _____. Many of his opponents have disappeared and some are certainly dead.

2. Karl seemed to be helping to plan the bank robbery, but in actual fact he was working _____ with the police and led them to the robbers.

3. It's all right. We don't need any extra help, thank you. We've got the situation _____ and we can deal with it ourselves.

4. This letter was delivered _____ for you this morning. There's no stamp on it.

5. At all major sporting events there are always ambulances and medics _____ in case someone is injured or falls ill.

6. I'm sorry. I don't have the information _____ at the moment. It'll take me a while to find it. Can you come back later this afternoon?

7. I showed my business plan to the bank, but they rejected it _____. They said that it would never work, but I've proved them completely wrong.

8. Your future is _____. Only you can decide what the best course of action is. Either you study hard and pass your exams, or you leave college.

9. Spring is such a lovely season, with all the birds singing, the flowers in bloom and young lovers strolling in the park, _____.

10. I don't really need your car, but I can take it _____ for £500. That's my only offer.

11. Cleopatra met her death _____. Legend says that she deliberately let a poisonous snake bite her.

12. The old king knew that his death was _____ and he might not last a week, so he called the royal family together for the last time.

9. Hand 2

Choose the correct phrase to go in the gaps in the sentences. You may have to change some forms to fit the sentences.

force one's hand, get one's hands off, get one's hands on, get out of hand, hand it to, hands are tied, have one's hands full, hold one's hand, keep a hand in, lend a hand, turn one's hand to, win hands down

1. You've got to _____ Jim. As a businessman, he knows a good deal when he sees one. He rarely gets things wrong and that's why he's so rich.

2. Hey! What do you think you're doing? That's my bag! _____ it.

3. I stopped teaching full time last year. I mostly write materials now, but I teach occasionally, just to _____, remember what to do and try out a few new ideas.

4. I'm really sorry, but I had to tell the boss about what you did on that business trip. He _____. He threatened to sack me if I didn't tell him.

5. I'd love to help you with the exam, but I'm afraid my _____. As the examiner, I'm not allowed to give the candidates any help at all.

6. Look. I can't _____ all your life. I've helped you a lot so far, but soon you'll have to start doing things for yourself and make your own decisions.

7. Phew! This box is really heavy! Can you _____ to lift it?

8. There are a lot of angry passengers waiting for their flight. We have to give them some assurances that they'll leave soon, or things are really going to

   _____.

9. Look at this! It's the latest high-definition digital video camera. I'd give anything to _____ that, but at £1000 it's impossible. I wish I had that money.

10. My boss is really upset. He thought he could play tennis better than me, but I _____, 6-0, 6-0.

11. Sorry. I can't come out tonight. I really _____ as I'm taking care of my own kids and my sister's kids. Another time perhaps.

12. You're a really skilful and clever person. I'm sure you can _____ any kind of work and do it really well.

10. Hand 3

Choose the correct word or phrase to go in the gaps in the sentences. You may have to change some forms to fit the sentences.

backhander, hand back, hand down, hand in, hand on, hand out, handout, hand over, hand round, hands-on, offhand, underhand

1. I don't trust Nigel. He's got a very _____ way of doing business. He'll lie and cheat as long as he makes money.

2. Has anybody _____ my college ID card? I think I must have left it in the library yesterday afternoon.

3. Jennifer's got a really _____ approach to running the business. She likes to be involved in everything and makes sure she knows what's happening.

4. Apparently, my employers got my tax code wrong and paid me too much, so I had to _____ more than £2000 to the taxman.

5. This wedding ring was _____ through the family to my mother, and then to me, so now it's my daughter's turn when she gets married on Saturday.

6. When the old Prime Minister finally retired, he _____ a strong economy and a strong currency to the next PM.

7. Khalid's going to retire after thirty years in the company, so I'm going to _____ a card to sign and an envelope to collect money.

8. I'm going to _____ these information sheets to you all. Can you all please keep them with you during the trip in case you get lost?

9. What's up with Marie? She was fine this morning, but she just spoke to me in a really _____ way, as if I'd done something wrong to upset her.

10. If you give the security guard a _____, say £20, he'll open the back door for you and let you in the concert.

11. I've been living on state _____ for over a year now, but I really want to get back to work and earn my own money.

12. The American police arrested the robbers, and they're going to _____ them _____ to our police when they arrive in America.

11. Hand 4

Choose the correct word or phrase to go in the gaps in the sentences. You may have to change some forms to fit the sentences.

first-hand, free hand, handbook, handbrake, handcuffs, handful, handmade, hand-picked, handshake, handspring, handwriting, heavy-handed

1. All the people in this squad were _____ by the commander, so they're the best soldiers for the job.
2. If you're not sure how to use this equipment, have a good look in the _____. It explains everything in detail.
3. Maria's got a really strong _____ for such a small person. My fingers are still hurting.
4. Remember. While the boss is away, I'm in charge of the daily running of the office. He's given me a _____ to do what I think is right, OK?
5. All these were _____ by skilled craftsmen in villages in the local area. Look at the quality.
6. Now, when you've put the engine in first gear, slowly release the _____ and move off, but keep looking out for traffic.
7. You really have to improve your _____ before the exam. The examiner won't be able to read your answers. I mean, what's this word here?
8. Thank heavens you're back at last. I've had enough of these children. They've been a real _____, running around and fighting all the time.
9. This book is a _____ account of the first ten years of the princess's marriage. The author worked as her manservant.
10. I've been training really hard in the gym and now I can do three _____ in a row. Watch me!
11. The last manager had such a _____ way of dealing with the players that they didn't want to play for him. They really hated the way he treated them.
12. The police caught the suspects and put them in _____ before taking them to the police station.

12. Hard 1

Choose the correct word or phrase to go in the gaps in the sentences. You may have to change some forms to fit the sentences.

hard-bitten, hard done by, hard-drinking, hard going, hard-hearted, hard hit, hard-hitting, hard-nosed, hard-pressed, hard pushed, hard-wearing, hard-working

1. I'm very pleased with Tim's progress at school this year. He's been extremely _____ and his coursework has been of a high standard.

2. You shouldn't be so _____. Other people aren't as fortunate as you and if they ask you for money, you have to be sympathetic and try to help.

3. Look. I'm really _____ at the moment. I've got so much work to finish that I just don't have any time to take on any more.

4. Pete's got a reputation as a wild, _____ hell-raiser, but when he's sober, he's actually a really nice person to know.

5. Jack's a real _____ businessman. He reached the top by always pushing for the best deal possible and not letting his emotions influence him.

6. The English exam was much more difficult than I thought it would be. I was _____ to finish it in time, but I just about managed it.

7. Motorists have been _____ by the latest rise in oil prices. They'll have to pay 10 pence more per litre.

8. I'd always wanted to climb Mount Everest, so it was great to get the chance to reach the top. It was really _____, but I managed it in the end.

9. I feel really sorry for the people who lost all their money when the company collapsed. They've been really _____. They didn't deserve it.

10. The film's about a _____ private detective who's seen and worked in the criminal underworld so long that he decides to get out, and that's when the trouble starts.

11. The former education minister gave a _____ interview on the evening news in which she severely criticised the government.

12. If you're going to go walking in the hills, put on a pair of _____ boots, because the ground is really rough.

13. Hard 2

Choose the correct word or phrase to go in the gaps in the sentences. You may have to change some forms to fit the sentences.

hard cash, hard copy, hard currency, hard disk, hard hat, hard-headed, hard labour, hard nut to crack, hard sell, hard shoulder, hardware, hard way

1. The car dealer wants £1000 in _____ by tomorrow morning or he'll sell the car to someone else. How are we going to get that kind of money?

2. There's something wrong with the car. I don't think we'll get to the next motorway service station, so I'll have to stop on the _____.

3. The police questioned the bank robbery suspect for three days. He was a _____, but in the end he had no choice but to confess to the crime.

4. If you don't have enough space to store everything on your computer's internal _____, you can buy an external one with 500Gb for only £50.

5. We can do all our shopping on the internet, so why do you want to do it the _____, pushing a trolley round the supermarket?

6. I got a phone call from a company selling new windows. They really tried to give me the _____, but I simply refused and put the phone down.

7. Can you go to the _____ store and buy me a new broom and mop? I need to clean the kitchen.

8. Reagan was convicted of armed robbery and sentenced to twenty years' _____. He spends most of his days breaking rocks.

9. When you go on the building site, you have to wear a _____ for protection because it's a very dangerous place.

10. I've finished the letter and saved it on the computer. Do you want me to print a _____ to send in the post now?

11. The banks in this country give you a bad exchange rate for your _____. You can get a much better rate on the black market.

12. My wife's very practical and _____ when it comes to money. She never wastes it on anything unnecessary, unlike me. I'm terrible with money.

14. Hard 3

Choose the correct word or phrase to go in the gaps in the sentences. You may have to change some forms to fit the sentences.

hard and fast, hard bargain, hardcore, harden, hard-left, hard-line, hard luck, hard of hearing, hardship, hard up, hardy, take it hard

1. I'm not giving you any more money. I worked really hard for it and I'm not going to let you play _____ with it and waste it all.

2. The tornado destroyed some houses in the street but left others intact. It was just our _____ that our house was in its path and got destroyed.

3. When I was young in the far north, we suffered a lot of _____, especially in winter when it snowed for five months and everything froze.

4. When you repair the broken plate, stick the two halves together and then leave it for at least an hour to allow the glue to _____ before you use it.

5. You drive a really _____. I thought that his asking price for the car was quite low and you wouldn't try to argue him down, but you did it well.

6. When Jenny's father died, she _____. It took a long time for her to start getting over it, but I don't think she really has yet. She's still really upset.

7. Can you lend me £100 till next week? I'm a bit _____ at the moment. I'll pay you back when I get my salary at the end of the month.

8. You see that café? That's where all the _____ bikers go to relax. They spend all their time looking at each other's latest motorbikes.

9. Despite being the first female president, she was a _____ politician who was never afraid to take difficult decisions and sack ministers if necessary.

10. These penguins are very _____ and can live in the Antarctic in conditions where the temperature regularly reaches minus 50C.

11. Tommy Bloor used to be a really _____ activist, but since being elected, he's moved much more to the political centre ground.

12. You'll have to speak louder to my grandmother. She'd very _____ these days. I think she's going deaf.

71

15. Hit

Choose the correct word or phrase to go in the gaps in the sentences. You may have to change some forms to fit the sentences.

hit-and-miss, hit-and-run, hit back, hit home, hit it off, hit list, hitman, hit on, hit out, hit the road, hit the roof, hit song

1. The problem with advertising products on TV is that it's so _____. You never know if your message gets through to the target audience.

2. Two men were seriously injured last night by a _____ driver. The police later found the car abandoned outside town with no sign of the driver.

3. I had to leave town and go into hiding. Jackson, the gang leader, had hired a _____ to kill me, because he thought I was a police informer.

4. While the family was waiting at the airport because of yet another delay, I _____ a great idea to amuse the children. Let me show you.

5. I've got a _____ of things that we need to do to the new house before we can go move into it, like repairing the roof and painting the house.

6. The Barcelona manager today _____ at his critics, who say that his tactics are not working. He blamed the number of injuries for the team's poor form.

7. And now, playing their latest _____, Don't Fight It, live for you today, we present to you the Flying Rocks! Let's hear it for them.

8. We'd better _____ again. We've got a long way to drive before we get to the campsite and it's going to get dark in a couple of hours.

9. I didn't really realise how much I'd miss my dog when he died. It really _____ when I went for a walk and he wasn't there to go with me.

10. Oh my gosh! Look at the mess! You'd better clean it up quick or your dad will _____ when he gets home.

11. Nadia met Bill at one of my parties. They _____ straight away, and now they're getting married. Isn't it lovely?

12. The opposition leader accused the prime minister of damaging the economy, but he _____, saying the previous government was to blame.

16. Hold 1

Choose the correct word or phrase to go in the gaps in the sentences. You may have to change some forms to fit the sentences.

foothold, get hold of, holdall, hold it against, hold one's own, hold together, hold-up, leasehold, on hold, take hold

1. In England people usually buy flats on a _____ basis, which means they own the right to live in the flat, but not the land that the flat is built on.

2. I've injected the anaesthetic. It'll take a few minutes to _____, and then you won't feel a thing.

3. It's a tough world out there. You need to learn to _____ and don't let anyone push you around.

4. Can you help me? I need to _____ £5000 by next week or I'll lose my house. I don't know how I can find that kind of money.

5. I went to the luggage shop and bought a new _____ to pack all my holiday clothes in.

6. When you make a cake you need to add plenty of butter to the pastry mix. Otherwise it won't _____ properly when you put it in the oven.

7. I know it was you who told the boss that I took the money. I just want you to know that I don't _____ you. It was my own fault and you did what you had to do.

8. Hello? Hello? Look, can I speak to the manager now? I've been on the phone _____ for the past ten minutes. It's just not acceptable.

9. My gosh! Look at the news. There's been a _____ at the bank. The police have shot two of the robbers and they've caught the others.

10. We're opening up a new office in China. If we can get a _____ in the Chinese market, it'll really increase our sales.

17. Hold 2

Choose the correct word or phrase to go in the gaps in the sentences. You may have to change some forms to fit the sentences.

hold back, hold down, hold off, hold on, hold out, hold over, hold up, hold with, uphold, withhold

1. I don't want you to see that boy again. He drinks and takes drugs, and I don't _____ that kind of behaviour.

2. It looks like it's going to rain, but I hope it _____ until all my washing is dry. Otherwise I'll have to bring it all in early.

3. It's very difficult to _____ a job these days. You never know how long a contract will last, or if your company will survive.

4. The job of the police is to _____ the law, keep the peace and investigate crime.

5. When you get your big chance to show how well you can play, don't _____. You have to try as hard as you can and give it all you've got.

6. Can you _____ for a few minutes? I've just got a bit of work to finish off and then we can go.

7. The soldiers fought bravely and _____ for three days, but finally the enemy proved too strong and broke their resistance.

8. My old employers want to _____ my final month's salary because they say I didn't give them enough notice to leave my job.

9. Because of the huge response to the competition, we've decided to _____ the closing date until next Friday, so keep sending your entries.

10. I'm sorry I'm late. My train got _____ at Manchester because of a problem with the signals.

18. Life 1

Choose the correct phrase to go in the gaps in the sentences. You do not have to change any forms to fit the sentences.

fight for life, for dear life, for life, for the life of, fright of one's life, larger than life, life and death, life and soul, life worth living, new lease of life

1. I went for a ride with Jeff on the back of his motorbike. It was really scary. He went so fast I was holding on _____.

2. Why don't you try to understand what I'm telling you? You have to help me or something terrible will happen. It's a matter of _____.

3. One of the passengers who were critically injured in last week's train crash has unfortunately lost his _____.

4. A man was jailed _____ today for the murder of Jenny Carson, who was found strangled at her home last December.

5. I just want to say that, although my father has died, we can all remember him with great fondness and love. He had so many friends and did so much for them. He was truly a _____ character.

6. After years of drug-taking, alcohol abuse and homelessness, Joe finally decided that his wasn't a _____, so he jumped in front of a train.

7. I'm so glad you invited Ingrid. She's so sociable and welcoming. She's the _____ of the party. Everyone wants to talk to her.

8. When I got home, I got the _____. The front door was open and there were noises upstairs. At first I thought they were burglars, but thankfully it was just my son and his friends back from university a week early.

9. The doctors told me today that there's no sign of the cancer any more. I'm so relieved. It's like a _____. I can't describe how good I feel.

10. I can't understand _____ me why Tom had to steal my money to pay his rent. He could have asked me and I'd have given it to him.

19. Life 2

Choose the correct word or phrase to go in the gaps in the sentences. You may have to change some forms to fit the sentences.

come to life, get a life, have a life, lay down one's life, life goes on, live life to the full, live one's life, risk life and limb, take a life, that's life

1. Hardly anyone arrived at the party at 9.00, and I was a bit worried, but then at around 10.00 my friends started arriving and the party really

   _____.

2. Now that I've retired, I've got lots of money saved up and the house is paid off, so I'm going to enjoy myself and _____.

3. We saw two kids at the bottom of the cliff with the sea coming in really fast. Keith climbed down and _____ to save them. He's really brave.

4. The greatest thing a soldier can do in battle is to _____ to save his comrade's.

5. If you _____ unlawfully, you must expect the severest punishment the law can give. You will go to prison for a minimum term of thirty years.

6. I was sure that Laughing Boy was the best horse and would win that race easily, but it came last and I lost £50. Oh well. _____!

7. I'm so fed up. I spend all day at work, and when I come home I have to clean, cook and take care of the kids. Then there's the shopping on the weekend. I really don't _____. It's got to change.

8. Look. I know you failed your exams and it's really upsetting, but you can't let it get you down. _____. You just pick yourself up and get on with it.

9. I don't believe it! You mean you made up this whole, stupid story just to annoy me? How can you be so childish? Just _____!

10. Leave me alone. If I want to spend my money on clothes and going out enjoying myself, that's my choice. Don't tell me how to _____.

20. Life 3

Choose the correct word or phrase to go in the gaps in the sentences. You may have to change some forms to fit the sentences.

lifebelt, lifeblood, life cycle, life form, lifelike, lifeline, life-size, lifespan, lifestyle, lifetime

1. Have you seen the cinema in the high street? They've put up a massive _____ model of King Kong for the film premiere.

2. I went to the new waxworks which opened in town yesterday. The models are so _____ that you expect them to move and talk to you.

3. Jim said that, although he had won £10 million in the lottery, he would not change his simple _____. He enjoyed it as it was.

4. The football academy is the _____ of this club. We get so many good young players coming through every year that it allows us to maintain our high standards.

5. Cicadas have a very strange _____. These insects hatch out of the egg and spend 17 years underground. Then they all turn into adults at the same time, come out, mate, lay their eggs and die.

6. Some scientists believe that there could be hundreds of planets in space with all kinds of strange _____ which are radically different from us.

7. Studies show that the average _____ in this country has increased by five years over the last century, mainly due to hygiene and healthcare improvements.

8. Our sports club would have closed without the money that the lottery fund gave us. It's been a real _____, and we're really grateful for it.

9. Look! There's some one who's fallen into the water. He can't swim. Quick! Throw him a _____.

10. I don't think governments can end world poverty quickly, at least not in my _____, and probably far longer.

WORD GROUPS

This section consists of twenty exercises dealing with groups of words with meanings relating to a particular concept, practice or topic. Each exercise has instructions for the completion of that particular exercise.

Contents

Notes on exercises

Word Groups Notes

1. Special uses of cardinal numbers
2. Special used of ordinal numbers

Certain numbers are used in set phrases and with colloquial and idiomatic meanings, and these exercises give practice in many of these uses.

3. Colour words referring to parts of the body

Certain colour words are used together with parts of the body to form different phrases. These phrases can have literal, abstract or often emotional meanings and these exercises give practice in many of these uses.

4. Gestures and facial expressions

This exercise practises verbs denoting various gestures and expressions, mostly to display emotions and attract attention.

5. Memory words

This exercise practises nouns, verbs and adjectives which express different aspects of memory, remembering and forgetting.

6. Verbs meaning *read* or *write*

This exercises practises verbs which express different ways of reading and writing and which relate to the purposes of reading and writing.

7. Body postures

This exercise practises verbs which extend the basic meanings of standing, sitting and lying, as well as other positions.

8. Travel verbs

This exercise practises verbs which express different ways of travelling by land, sea or air. Some of the verbs are more usually encountered as nouns, and others can also be used as nouns.

9. Streets and roads

This exercises practises nouns which refer to different types of roads and streets, or parts of roads, both in and out of cities and towns.

10. Print media

This exercises practises nouns which refer to different types of writing and people associated with print media, such as newspapers, books and magazines.

11. Geographical features 1
12. Geographical features 2

These exercises practise nouns which refer to various features of land, sea and inland water.

13. Shopping and buying things

This exercises practises nouns and verbs which express different aspects of shopping and different ways of buying and paying for things.

14. Computer words
15. Internet and related areas

These exercises practise important words related to computing and using the internet, some of which are relatively recent or specialised.

16. Weather

This exercise practises words which refer to more specific and descriptive aspects of the weather.

17. Tastes and smells

This exercises practises nouns, verbs and adjectives which express various positive and negative aspects of taste and smell. Some of the words can be used in more than one way, and this is indicated in the answers.

18. Money 1
19. Money 2

These exercises practise nouns, verbs and adjectives which refer to different forms of money, and different ways of using and referring to money, both legal and illegal.

20. Water words

This exercises practises nouns and verbs referring to different forms that water takes, and different ways it moves and can be used.

1. Special uses of cardinal numbers

Choose the correct phrase to go in the gaps in the sentences. You may have to change some forms to fit the sentences.

foursquare, high five, one-and-only, one by one, one-dimensional, one-off, one-sided, one-way, ten a penny, two-faced, two-time, two-way

1. England played well and scored five goals, but the match was far too _____, because the other team played so badly.

2. Every time the volleyball team win a point, they all give each other _____ to celebrate. It's like they've won the game each time.

3. Because they had worked so hard during the sales week, all the store's sales staff got a _____ bonus payment of £200 each.

4. Tonight, we present to you the greatest singing star in history of the world, the _____ Michael Jackson! Let's hear it for him!

5. Jenny's really upset. She found out that her husband was _____ her with another woman. She says she's going to leave him.

6. I liked the action and the plot in the film, but I felt the characters were a bit _____ and not realistic or interesting enough.

7. After the armed police had surrounded the bank, the six robbers came out _____ with their hands on their heads.

8. We know that you're having a difficult time, but we're all standing _____ behind you and we'll support you to the end.

9. There's no point in going down that road. It's a _____ street. You'll have to go round and come back up.

10. Don't believe a word Jo says. She'll tell you one thing and tell me something completely different. She's the most _____ person I've ever met

11. I remember when mobile phones cost hundreds of pounds, but you can get cheap ones everywhere now. They're _____ in London.

12. You have to work hard together with your wife to make your marriage work. It's a _____ process, with a lot of give and take.

2. Special uses of ordinal numbers

Choose the correct number to go in the gaps in the sentences. Some are used more than once.

first, second, third, fifth, sixth, seventh, eleventh

1. If you propose the new financial plan at the meeting, I'll _____ the proposal. I'm sure the others will vote for it.

2. The ruling party believed that there was a _____ column in the organisation trying to destabilise it and take over, so they began a huge purge.

3. I don't want you to tell me what Maria has decided to do. I want to hear it _____-hand from her. She needs to explain her reasons to me.

4. If you fly to America, you should take New American Airways. Their in-flight service is _____-rate, the best I've ever had.

5. Have you tried that excellent new Italian restaurant on Bond Street? Their lasagne is _____ to none. It's the best I've ever tasted.

6. I'm not going to agree to the intervention of any _____ party. This matter is between only you and me, and doesn't concern anyone else.

7. I know you really like my car, so when I'm ready to sell it, I'll give you _____ refusal before I ask anyone else.

8. My son Freddie really loves swimming in the sea. He swims like a fish. It's _____ nature to him.

9. The workers were about to strike, but at the _____ hour the management agreed to pay them more, so they called it off at the last moment.

10. I'll have a beer with my dinner. Actually, on _____ thoughts I'll have mineral water, as I'm driving.

11. It's funny how some animals can feel an earthquake before it happens. It's as if they have a _____ sense that we humans don't have.

12. I opened the letter with my exam results and saw that I got three A grades. It was fantastic. I was in _____ heaven.

3. Colour words referring to parts of the body

Choose the correct colour to go in the gaps in the sentences. Some are used more than once.

black, blue, green, purple, red, white

1. The thief claimed that he didn't steal the diamond ring, but he was caught
    _____-handed on the security video in the jewellery shop.

2. When my next-door neighbour saw my new sports car, his face went
    _____ with envy. You could see he really wanted one of his own.

3. Jennifer claims that she's related to the royal family, but she hasn't got a drop of
    _____ blood in her body. There's no way she's related to them.

4. The plane skidded on landing and shook violently. Everybody was trembling and
    _____-faced with fear when they got off.

5. After the boxing match Johnny was ecstatic that he had won, even though his
    face was beaten _____ and _____.

6. I don't understand how Stan can make his garden look so nice. He really must
    have _____ fingers. He really knows how to take care of plants.

7. Rugby is played by tough, _____-blooded men. If you play it, you
    need a lot of aggression and you should expect to be injured from time to time.

8. The problem with Joey is that, as far as his mother is concerned, he can do
    nothing wrong. He's her perfect, _____-eyed boy.

9. Penny grabbed this guy from behind and squeezed him in a big hug. Imagine
    how _____-faced and embarrassed she was when he turned
    round, and she realised it wasn't her boyfriend, but a total stranger. We all
    laughed so much!

10. I kicked my ball through the neighbour's window, and he came charging out
    shouting at me. His face was _____with rage, so I just turned
    and ran.

4. Gestures and facial expressions

Choose the correct gesture or expression to go in the gaps in the sentences. Make sure you put them in the correct form where necessary.

drum, fidget, grin, light up, nudge, pat, poke, scowl, sneer, squint, stroke, tap

1. Jimmy started falling asleep in the middle of the film, so I _____ him with my elbow to wake him up, but he just fell asleep again.

2. You shouldn't _____ at people just because you think you're better than them. One day you'll regret it, when someone does the same to you.

3. I was just standing in the street smoking, when this guy came right up to me, _____ me in the chest with his finger and told me to stop.

4. Alex was so pleased when he realised that he had got the job. Everyone shook his hand and _____ him on the back in congratulation.

5. Roger sat at the table with all the papers spread out in front of him, _____ his long beard as he thought about what to do.

6. I was standing at the bus stop when someone _____ me on the shoulder. I turned and saw Kelly, my old girlfriend from university.

7. All the photographers rushed to get a picture as Jackson came out of his house, but he just _____ angrily at them as he went to get in his car.

8. Jo stood on the podium holding her gold medal and _____ broadly in sheer delight. All her dreams had come true at that moment.

9. Fred _____ as he came out of the dark room into the bright sunshine. It took a few minutes for his eyes to get used to it.

10. Terry just sat _____ his fingers impatiently on the table as he waited for the call that would shape his future. Had he got the job?

11. Can you stop _____ with your keys? It's really annoying. If you're bored, go and play outside on your bike or something.

12. When I came home, little Jenny was sitting in the corner by herself looking really sad, but her face _____ when I gave her the new kitten.

5. Memory words

Choose the correct memory word to go in the gaps in the sentences. Make sure you put them in the correct form where necessary.

amnesia, forgettable, forgetful, memorable, memorial, memorise, mindful, recall, recollection, remind, reminisce, souvenir

1. When I was young, I don't _____ exactly how old I was, I went to live with my grandparents in Trinidad. It was a wonderful, carefree time for me.

2. Alex can remember everything up to the moment of the accident, but he has no _____ of what happened after. His mind's completely blank.

3. If you want to get a good grade in your literature exam, you need to _____ some important quotes from the set books and use them.

4. That house _____ me of the one I lived in as a boy. It has the same design and appearance, even the same colour.

5. The government decided to build a fountain in the park as a _____ to Princess Diana, who used to live nearby before she died.

6. Last week I met my old school friend, Helen. We had dinner together and _____ about the days we spent together at school.

7. We had over 500 people at my sister's wedding. We all had a great time. It was a really _____ occasion. I'll show you the photos if you want.

8. Before I left France to come home after spending three months studying, my host family gave me a watch as a _____ of my stay with them.

9. We planned a great day out at the seaside, but the car broke down, it rained all day and we had no food. It was a completely _____ trip.

10. How can you be so _____? All I asked you to do was to take the dinner out of the freezer, and you didn't. Now we've got nothing to eat!

11. We should be _____ of the people who fought and died for the freedom of this country. That's why there's a special day for them in November.

12. When the police eventually found Penny she was suffering from severe _____. She couldn't even remember her name.

6. Verbs meaning *read* or *write*

Choose the correct verb to go in the gaps in the sentences. Make sure you put them in the correct form where necessary.

browse, engrave, jot, look over, overwrite, proofread, record, scan, scribble, skim, transcribe, type

1. I didn't have time to read the whole article in detail. I just _____ through it quickly and got a general idea of what it's about.

2. Samuel Pepys carefully _____ in his diary everything he did on a daily basis. That's why it's such an important historical document.

3. If you hold the paper up to the light and look at the text carefully, you can see that the original text was _____ when the paper was reused.

4. I can hardly read his writing. It's like he just had a few moments to quickly _____ the message before he left.

5. The trophy has the names of all the winning teams _____ on it, and our team is going to be the next.

6. At the airport I quickly _____ the big departure screen to find out when my flight was leaving, but it wasn't there. It had been cancelled.

7. Ellie, you're the fastest of all of us with a computer, so I'll dictate the letter and you can _____ it.

8. I love visiting bookshops and _____ the shelves for anything interesting to buy. It's a great way to pass the time.

9. I've got an interesting new job. I have to listen to the news on the radio and _____ it to put on the internet.

10. After a writer submits a manuscript, your job is to _____ it and correct any mistakes in spelling, punctuation and so on.

11. Have you got a pen? I just need to _____ down this phone number.

12. Can you _____ my story for me and tell me if you think it's worth sending it to a publisher? I'd be really grateful if you could.

7. Body postures

Choose the correct verb to go in the gaps in the sentences. Make sure you put them in the correct form where necessary.

bow, cower, crouch, curl up, kneel, lean, perch, pose, recline, sit up, slouch, slump

1. When you say your prayers in church, you have to _____, because it shows respect and reverence.

2. The game was so exciting that we were all _____ on the ends of our seats, ready to jump up as soon as the ball went into the net.

3. The hunter _____ down with his rifle behind the tree, like a tiger ready to jump on its prey. As the deer approached, he took aim and fired.

4. The great thing about travelling business class on a flight is that you can make your chair go right down to _____ when you sleep.

5. Remember, when you're about to fight in karate, you should _____ to your opponent out of respect, but always keep your eyes on him or her.

6. When the teacher banged on the blackboard, all the children _____ straight in their seats and started to pay attention.

7. The children were so tired after the trip today they just _____ on the sofa in front of the TV and went to sleep. I had to carry them up to bed.

8. There were some boys standing around on the street corner. One of them was _____ against the wall and blocking the pavement.

9. The police found a car in the middle of the road, with the driver _____ over the steering wheel. He was completely drunk.

10. Tom could see the shape of a man with a gun through the glass door, so he went and _____ under the desk, hoping he would go away.

11. You really shouldn't _____ on your chair like that. You should learn to sit correctly or you're going to get back problems.

12. As the film stars went into the cinema for the premiere, they stopped on the red carpet and _____ for photographs. They all looked so vain!

8. Travel verbs

Choose the correct verb to go in the gaps in the sentences. Make sure you put them in the correct form where necessary.

commute, cruise, ferry, fly, hitchhike, journey, migrate, motor, ride, tour, transport, voyage

1. In the past, the peasants used to _____ into the mountains with their livestock in the summer, and back into the lowlands for the winter.

2. This summer, we're not going abroad for our holiday. We've decided to take the car and _____ Scotland for a month instead.

3. When I was a poor student, I used to _____ from home to university to save money. I often had to wait in the rain for ages before I got a lift.

4. Before they built the bridge connecting this island to the mainland, there was a boat to _____ cars over, but it's gone now, which is a real pity!

5. We've saved up enough money for a really expensive holiday. We're flying to Greece to _____ the islands in a luxury yacht. I can't wait to go.

6. The great thing about these country roads is that you can _____ along at high speed, without any traffic lights or roundabouts.

7. I used to _____ into the centre of London every day, but I got so fed up with the dirty, crowded trains that I mostly work from home now.

8. The quickest way from London to Paris used to be to _____, but now the train under the Channel is just as quick and far more comfortable.

9. I'd love to _____ round the world in a sailing boat, like the explorers of old, discovering new lands and peoples.

10. There are so many cycle paths in and out of town now that the fastest, cheapest and healthiest way to get around is to _____ a bike.

11. The company uses articulated lorries to _____ the goods across country to the main depot, and small vans to deliver the goods to the shops.

12. When we went to France last summer, we didn't have any kind of travel plan. We just _____ around the country in whatever ways we could.

9. Streets and roads

Choose the correct word to go in the gaps in the sentences. Make sure you put them in the plural where necessary.

avenue, crossroads, dead-end, flyover, junction, lane (2), motorway, pass, roundabout, route, slip-road, tunnel, underpass

1. What I really enjoy in the summer is to drive along those lovely, little, winding country _____ and stop for lunch in a village pub.

2. We've bought a really nice house on the edge of town. It's on this beautiful, wide _____, lined with big trees. It's a lovely area.

3. I've found a great website for drivers to plan their holidays. It showed me three different _____ to get from Paris to Rome.

4. I don't like driving on the _____. Everyone drives too fast and you get really tired and bored, because it's so monotonous. I prefer smaller roads.

5. Ever since they built the new _____ here, you can just drive up quickly and down the other side, and avoid all the traffic below.

6. This _____ is so short that you don't need to turn your lights on to go through it. You can see the light at the other end.

7. When we were on holiday in Switzerland, we drove over a _____ at 2000 metres. The views across the mountains and valleys were fantastic.

8. Ever since they built the _____ under the sea from England to France, it's been far quicker to get there than by ferry.

9. We're leaving this road at the next _____, so we need to get into the left _____ now so that we can get onto the _____ easily.

10. Slow down now because we're coming to a _____. If there's nothing coming, you can continue round and take the first right.

11. Where do I go at the _____? Left, right or straight ahead?

12. We'll have to turn round and come out again. This road's a _____.

10. Print media

Choose the correct word to go in the gaps in the sentences. Make sure you put them in the plural where necessary.

article, column, comment, correspondent, critic, editor, gossip, journalist, periodical, press, publisher, review

1. Have you heard? Jim's off to New York next week. He's going to be our newspaper's new American _____.

2. Have you read the _____ of your new film in the newspapers? The _____ really love it! It's definitely going to be a big hit!

3. I've finished writing my first novel. Now I'm looking for a _____ to send it to. Do you know any that take on new writers?

4. A truly open, democratic society guarantees freedom of the _____, although it doesn't mean that newspapers can print whatever they want.

5. The news _____ really likes my story about the lion which escaped from the zoo. He's going to run it on the front page in tomorrow's paper.

6. It's sometimes difficult to distinguish true political reporting from political _____ in many newspapers these days.

7. Lots of sportsmen and women write a weekly _____ in a newspaper these days, where they talk about their training and give their opinions on sport.

8. Have you read the _____ in today's paper about the latest dance craze from America? All the young people are doing it.

9. The problem with a lot of papers these days is that they prefer to print _____ about celebrities and film stars, and not enough real news.

10. "Science News" is a first class new monthly _____, which explores the latest developments in modern science and technology.

11. Most people think that _____ only tell lies and make up stories to sell their newspapers. Few people trust them to tell the truth.

11. Geographical features 1

Choose the correct word to go in the gaps in the sentences. Make sure you put them in the plural where necessary.

archipelago, channel, cliff, desert, estuary, glacier, jungle, ocean, plain, range, valley, waterfall

1. The _____ makes its way slowly down the mountainside, until it melts and becomes the source of the River Rhine.

2. After the Mayan civilisation fell, all the great cities and buildings were gradually covered in dense _____, until they totally disappeared from view.

3. The Andes is the longest mountain _____ in the world, stretching from the Caribbean down to the bottom of South America.

4. The whole country of Indonesia consists of a vast _____ of over 10,000 islands, from tiny islets to giants, like Sumatra.

5. This river meets the sea in a huge _____ twenty kilometres long and fifty kilometres wide, which is an important habitat for migrating birds.

6. The island is separated from the mainland by a narrow _____, which is very difficult to cross because of its dangerous currents.

7. You might think that this _____ is so hot and dry that few animals can live there, but some animals, like snakes and scorpions, manage to survive..

8. In the summer, the herdsmen take their cattle up the mountain for the fresh grass, but return to the _____ in the autumn.

9. Every year the salmon swim up the river to their breeding grounds, even jumping up fast-flowing _____ on the way.

10. The Pacific is the largest _____ in the world, stretching from America to Asia.

11. The flat land at the foot of the mountain stretches away for hundreds of miles in a vast, almost treeless _____, covered in long grass.

12. Be careful as you walk along here. Don't go too close to the edge of the _____. It's a two-hundred metre drop down to the sea.

12. Geographical features 2

Choose the correct word to go in the gaps in the sentences. Make sure you put them in the plural where necessary.

coastline, continent, forest, headland, inlet, lake, swamp, peninsula, plateau, ravine, region, volcano

1. The river flows down the mountain and into an extremely narrow and deep _____. After about ten kilometres, it flows out into a wide plain.

2. As you walk up the mountain, the thick _____ gradually thins out, until there are no trees left after about 2000 metres.

3. The _____ is joined to the mainland by a narrow strip of land less than a kilometre wide.

4. Antarctica is the only _____ in the world where there are no land animals living there all year round.

5. The whole of country of Tibet is a vast _____ over 5000 metres in height, stretching for hundreds of miles. It's known as the Roof of the World.

6. The railway follows the _____ for about fifty miles, passing through seaside towns and giving you wonderful sea views.

7. Up on this _____, there used to be a tall lighthouse, which would warn ships to keep clear of the rocks down below.

8. The captain sailed along the coast looking for a sheltered _____ where he could anchor the boat safely for a few days and avoid the big storm.

9. Scientists studying this _____ are worried that the increased smoke and activity are signs that it might erupt any day now.

10. The main _____ affected by hurricanes are the Caribbean and the south eastern US, but hurricanes occasionally reach as far as New York.

11. Although the Caspian Sea contains salt water, it is actually the largest _____ in the world, as it's not connected to any other sea.

12. The river flows so slowly that it turns the land into a huge _____, full of crocodiles, frogs, snakes and other creatures which inhabit wetlands.

13. Shopping and buying things

Choose the correct word to go in the gaps in the sentences. Make sure you put them in the correct form where necessary.

balance, bargain, cost, deposit, discount, exchange, instalment, offer, order, purchase, receipt, refund, sale, value

1. In the past the _____ usually started the day after Christmas, but now many shops have them before Christmas, with big reductions.

2. If the goods are faulty you can return them. You can _____ them for something else, or we can _____ your money. In any case, you must bring the _____ with you as proof of your

    _____.

3. If you like, you can pay for the computer in full now. Alternatively, you can put down a _____ and either pay the _____ when you come to collect it, or pay it off in twelve monthly _____.

4. You can go to the store to buy this digital camera, but if you place your _____ online, we will give you a _____ of 10%.

5. Sometimes shops sell goods below _____ price, which means that they effectively lose money when they sell them.

6. Whenever I go shopping I always look at the quality of a product, but it has to be at the right price, or you don't get _____ for money.

7. I'll give you £500 for your old car as part exchange for the new one. That's my best _____. Take it or leave it.

8. Look at my new flat-screen TV. I only paid £100 for it at my local electric store. It was a real _____. You won't find it cheaper anywhere else.

14. Computer words

Choose the correct word or phrase to go in the gaps in the sentences. Make sure you put them in the correct form where necessary.

application, hard drive, hardware, input, keyboard, log on, memory, monitor, operating, output, processor, software, storage, upgrade

1. Make sure that any new _____, like a scanner or a printer, is correctly connected to your computer, or it may not work.

2. We usually _____ data into a computer through typing it on the _____ or scanning it, and then _____ it through the _____ and printer.

3. The biggest form of _____, where you can save your data on a computer, is the _____, but you can also use a floppy disk or memory stick to take it with you.

4. All computers use an _____ system for users to work with and every so often you can get an _____ for the system to make it work faster and better.

5. When you buy a new _____ to use on your computer, make sure that it's compatible with the system you're using, or it won't work.

6. If you buy this latest computer model, we also give you a free package of the latest video and office _____, already loaded and ready for you to use.

7. When you enrol in the college you will get a user name and password, which will allow you to _____ to the college computer system.

8. When you buy a new computer, remember to check the speed of the _____ as well as the size of the _____, since both can affect the computer's ability to function fast and well.

15. Internet and related areas

Choose the correct word or phrase to go in the gaps in the sentences. Make sure you put them in the plural where necessary.

auction, attachment, blog, browser, click, download, firewall, link, phishing, search engine, spam, surf, upload, virus

1. Email is a great way of sending messages quickly, but there's far too much

   _____, which is just rubbish and has to be deleted.

2. Never open an email _____ unless you know who sent it to you.

   You may get a _____, which can damage your computer.

3. My new broadband connection is so fast I can _____ large files

   from the internet in a few seconds, and _____ files to my website

   almost as fast.

4. I'm writing a daily _____ about my journey round the world. Lots of

   people read it every day and comment on it, usually very positively.

5. Before you install your broadband internet connection, make sure you have a

   _____ to prevent online criminals gaining access your computer.

6. This is the only _____ I use these days. It finds hundreds of

   websites really quickly, and organises the results really well.

7. I put my old game system on an online _____. I sold it in one day

   for the final price of £100.

8. If the mouse pointer goes over a word or picture and it changes to a hand, then

   you know it's a _____ and you can _____ on it with

   the mouse to go to another page.

9. Never reply to a _____ email, which asks you for your bank

   details. They're sent by criminals who want to gain access to your account.

10. If you use the latest version of this web _____, you'll find it much

    faster and easier to _____ the internet.

16. Weather

Choose the correct word to go in the gaps in the sentences. Make sure you put them in the correct form where necessary.

blizzard, breeze, depression, downpour, drought, flood, gale, heatwave, humidity, hurricane, snowdrift, squall

1. As soon as I got in the car it started raining really hard. It was a real _____ and in just a few minutes, the whole street was _____ under half a metre of water.

2. This is what I love about summer. You can sit in the warm sunshine with a gentle _____ blowing to keep you cool.

3. It's almost the end of the month and it still hasn't rained. If it goes on like this there's going to be a _____.

4. The American government has warned residents of Miami to leave the city by tonight, as there's a very powerful _____ on its way.

5. The temperature has been over 40 degrees Celsius for a week now, but the _____ is going to continue for a few days before it cools down.

6. When we were coming down from the mountain, we were caught in a fierce _____ and had to shelter in a cave. When it finally stopped, everything was completely white and there were _____ up to three metres deep.

7. There's a real _____ blowing outside. I had to really fight to stop myself falling over and stay on my feet.

8. The deep _____ currently moving over the country means there's going to be a lot of rain over the next 24 hours.

9. When we were out on the boat, the wind got up and it started raining. Luckily, it was just a short _____ and not a big storm. The wind stopped and the sun soon came out again.

10. The worst thing about living in a tropical city like Jakarta is the _____. It's so high that as soon as you go outside, you start sweating, and it stays on your body all the time.

17. Tastes and smells

Choose the correct word to go in the gaps in the sentences. Make sure you put them in the correct form where necessary.

acrid, aroma, bitterness, bland, odour, pungent, savour, scent, smack, sniff, stink, stench, tang, whiff

1. When you taste the wine, keep it on your tongue for a few moments to
   _____ all the different flavours.

2. I opened the bin and found rotten meat in it. The _____ was so
   overpowering that I felt sick and I quickly closed it.

3. I love going to markets when I'm travelling. There are so many different
   _____ in the air, some of them completely new.

4. Most people add lots of sugar to lemon juice to sweeten it, but I like the
   _____ of freshly squeezed lemons.

5. Although the escaped prisoners had been on the run for an hour, the dogs soon
   picked up their _____ and tracked them down.

6. I hate going into the Johnsons' house. It really _____ of cigarettes
   because they smoke all day long.

7. The restaurant kitchen was filled with the wonderful _____ of the
   spices being cooked in the food.

8. As we approached the volcano, we _____ the air. The
   _____ smell of the smoke and fumes was getting stronger.

9. I love that very slight _____ of spring that you can get when you go
   outside at the beginning of March, just as the trees come into blossom.

10. I had dinner in that new restaurant last night. The food wasn't bad, just a bit
    _____, that's all. It needed more herbs and spices.

11. During the church ceremony, the _____ smoke of the burning
    incense filled the air.

12. I don't like food which really _____ of chilli sauce. I like just a
    little to add a slight _____ to the food.

18. Money words 1

Choose the correct word to go in the gaps in the sentences. Make sure you put them in the correct form where necessary.

bet, bill, change, coin, currency, economise, exchange, expenditure, finance, fraud, mint, note, rate, tax

1. Before I travel abroad I always go to the post office to get my foreign
   _____. You can get a much better _____ of
   _____ than they offer in the banks at the airport.

2. Damn! I haven't got any one-pound _____ to put in the parking
   meter. I'll have to go to a shop and see if they can give me _____
   for a ten-pound _____.

3. I made a £100 _____ with John that Brazil would beat Germany in
   the World Cup final and I won! He was really annoyed at losing the money to
   me.

4. You have to pay _____ on anything that you buy in the shops
   here, but you can claim it back at the airport when you leave the country.

5. I'd like one thousand dollars in one-hundred dollar _____, please.

6. One thing you have to learn in life is to _____ if you want to have
   enough money for everything. Don't spend too much and save up if you want to
   buy something expensive.

7. The police arrested Jack and charged him with _____. They found
   hundreds of fake credit cards in his house.

8. I'm saving money for my son to go to university. I want to make sure he has the
   _____ to study for three years before he starts his course.

9. There's far too much money going out of the company and not enough coming
   in. We have to find ways to cut our _____, like using less electricity
   and saving paper.

10. This old building is where the country's _____ used to be three
    hundred years ago. It closed because it couldn't produce enough money fast
    enough to go into circulation.

19. Money words 2

Choose the correct word to go in the gaps in the sentences. Make sure you put them in the correct form where necessary.

bribe, budget, cash, credit, debit, debt, duty, economical, embezzle, income, interest, mercenary, outgoings, wager

1. Today in parliament the Finance Minister presented his _____ for the next year. He announced that he had increased _____ on cigarettes by 5 pence and on alcohol by 10 pence.
2. People are so _____ these days. They won't do anything unless you pay them. When I was young we did each other favours for nothing.
3. I'll make a _____ with you. Whoever scores less in the quiz has to buy the other one dinner. Is it a deal?
4. Can you hang on a minute? I need to go to the _____ machine and get some money out.
5. If your _____, for example your salary and savings, is less than your _____, like your rent and bills, then you're going to get into _____, which is not a good idea.
6. Until my salary goes in at the end of the month, my bank account is usually in _____, but it's in _____ now because I got a big bonus from work. Let's celebrate!
7. You should learn to be more _____ with your money and not spend so much on going out. You need to save for university.
8. I'm going to move my savings to another account to get a higher rate of _____ on them.
9. When the accountant examined the company's bank account, they found over £1 million missing. The manager had _____ it over two years and left the country, and now the police can't find him.
10. In some countries, government officials won't do anything unless you pay them a _____. It's illegal, but it's just the way they do things.

20. Words relating to water

Choose the correct word to go in the gaps in the sentences. Make sure you put them in the correct form where necessary.

brine, condensation, damp, drain, evaporate, gush, moisten, rainfall, rinse, soak, steam, trickle

1. When you _____ the stamp to stick on the letter, use just a little water or it won't stick properly.

2. When it rains in the desert, the water usually _____ very quickly because of the intense heat.

3. There's still soap in these clothes. You'll have to _____ them again in the washing machine to get it all out.

4. After the pasta has boiled, make sure you _____ the water out of it before you add the sauce.

5. Fish is often tinned in _____, because the salt in the water helps to preserve it and give it flavour.

6. The problem with driving in the cold and rain is that you get too much _____ on the inside of the windows and you can't see well.

7. When the pipe broke, the water _____ out like a fountain and completely covered the road.

8. If the toaster gets dirty, wipe it down with a _____ cloth, but don't put it directly in water.

9. When the hot lava from the volcano hit the sea, the water boiled and clouds of _____ rose up into the sky.

10. The annual _____ is so low in this part of the country it's amazing that any animals can live here at all.

11. Usually this river is quite full and flows quite strongly, but because we've had hardly any rain lately, it's become just a _____.

12. If the clothes are very dirty, leave them to _____ overnight in soap and water before you put them through their normal wash.

WORD PLAYS AND GAMES

This section consists of twenty exercises with word plays consisting of missing letters and word associations. The word plays entitled Vagrant Vowels and Recalcitrant Consonants feature on eflworksheets.com, though the exercises here play with different words. The other word plays entitled Double-ups and One Way or Another, are introduced here for the first time.

In exercises with Recalcitrant Consonants and Vagrant Vowels, there are some words which have either a missing letter or an extra one, thereby creating a new word, for example, *beat - bet* or *scream - cream*. The learner has to read the text carefully to identify the words in question and decide how to change the word. This may involve adding a letter or removing one. In some exercises, the letter is the same one for each word, for example, *scream - cream, smile - mile*, whereas in others the learner has to find a different letter for each word identified. The idea here is to help learners check written work carefully for mistakes, as well as to amuse them and increase their vocabulary.

The main aim of the exercises entitled One Way or Another is to look at word combinations which can have either word first or second in the combination. For example, if we take the words *back* and *date*, we can make the combinations *backdate* and *date back*. The combinations may be compounds written as one word, as in *backdate* or as two words, as in *date back*. In each case the meaning of the combinations is invariably different.

The main aim of the exercises with Double-ups is to provide practice in forming compound words, especially nouns and verbs. In each case there are three words which are used to create two different compounds, with one of the words "doubling up" as the second element of the first compound, and the first element of the second compound. For example, the three words *street, car* and *sick* can make two compounds: *streetcar* and *carsick*. The learner may have to supply the "double-up" word, for example, *street_____sick*, or the first and last words, for example _____*car_____*. Each compound word has a definition to help the learner work it out.

Each activity has a short explanation at the beginning outlining exactly what learners needs to do. They should be read carefully before the exercise is attempted.

Contents

1. Recalcitrant consonants 1: extra *r* or *l*

In this text there are twelve words with an extra letter. Seven have an extra *r* and five have an extra *l*. Underline each word in the text and write the new word in the list at the bottom.

Dead Easy – a Crime Story

Crime friction is the latest popular trend in books. I think it's the most exciting type of writing around. I read a really great book the other day called Dead Easy. It was written with a lot of tension, excitement and flair. It takes place in Italy with two political fractions who come together to commit a blank robbery for reasons too complicated to explain here.

The bland of robbers set up a clamp in a shred outside a town and spend two weeks making their plans. Then one night under cover of a thick flog they creep into the town to carry out the crime. One of the criminals has managed to get hold of a flake identity as a security guard, and he unlocks the door to let them in. While they are grabbing the money, because of their sloppy planning, they don't realise that the guard was actually planted by the police and trips them off that the robbers are there.

Anyway, to cut a long story short, the crops arrive and there's a big gun fright. The robbers' hopeless situation is plain; their plot has failed, and soon there are a lot of them lying dread on the floor. However, a few of them escape, and that's when it starts to get really interesting as the relationships between them become strained. The climax is really breathtaking and there's on final twist. Go out and claim your copy now. You won't be disappointed.

---

1. _____ ; 2. _____ ; 3. _____ ;

4. _____ ; 5. _____ ; 6. _____ ;

7. _____ ; 8. _____ ; 9. _____ ;

10. _____ ; 11. _____ ; 12. _____

2. Recalcitrant consonants 2: missing *r* or *l*

In this text there are ten words which are missing a letter. Five have an *r* missing and five have an *l* missing. However, each of the ten words can take either an *l* or an *r* to make another word, so you have to choose which new word is correct, e.g.: *cam - clam - cram*. Underline each word in the text and write the new word in the list at the bottom.

House Proud

People everywhere are becoming more and more house-proud. When they invite guests, they don't want them to get a fight when they come in the door and see a mess. They want to show how well-kept their houses are. If you are one of these people, here are some tips which can make sure your house is always in top condition to show off to visitors. They don't even cost a lot if you have only a little money to pay with.

If your windows are cracked, it's a good idea to get someone to gaze them professionally. Some companies do this for fee if you allow them to showcase your house.

When you decorate your rooms, choose your colours carefully. If the colours cash, it will give your visitors a negative impression. If you have pictures on the wall, you can find some attractive fames to put them in. Lighting is also very important. Don't just use a standard ceiling light, but position other lights around the room. You can even get ones which camp onto a bookcase or table.

Finally, before your guests arrive make sure your house is clean and smells nice. Vacuum-clean your carpets and sweep wooden floors with a soft boom. In the kitchen and bathroom, use a cleaner with strong beach and some air freshener. It's worth spending a little more on a good band. If you do all these things, your guests are sure to appreciate it and tell you so.

---

1. _____ ; 2. _____ ; 3. _____ ;

4. _____ ; 5. _____ ; 6. _____ ;

7. _____ ; 8. _____ ; 9. _____ ;

10. _____

3. Recalcitrant consonants 3: missing *s* or *c*

In this text there are twelve words missing a letter. Eight have an *s* missing and four have a *c* missing, and in each case they combine with *h* to make either *sh* or *ch*. Underline each word in the text and write the new word in the list at the bottom.

A Lucky Break to Love

I'll always remember how I met my husband. It was in a December, just before the Christmas holiday. I remember it because it was really hilly. I was hungry, but there was no food in the house, so I went round to the fish and hip hop and got a nice hot haddock meal. When I got home again I had a bit of a hock. The door was hut, but I didn't have my keys. Then I remembered - I had left them in the hall.

I put the food on the ground and went round the back to see if I could climb in the bathroom window. I put the ladder against the wall and started to climb up. I used my hoe to try to hammer on the window latch to loosen it, but I hit it too hard and managed to hatter the window pane. Unfortunately, I was hurt by a harp hard of glass and my hand started bleeding.

Just then, a policeman who was passing heard me scream and asked what I was doing. I came down and told him, and when he saw my hand he immediately bound it up with his hankie, climbed up into the bathroom and let me in. He washed and bound the wound, as he knew first aid.

Then I asked him if he wanted to stay for something to eat, so I gave him a hare of my dinner and we had a nice long hat. He was really harming and I really liked him. After he was sure I was OK, he left, but came round the next day to check on me, and the rest is history. We've been together for twelve years now and we're still so happy.

---

1. _____ ; 2. _____ ; 3. _____ ;

4. _____ ; 5. _____ ; 6. _____ ;

7. _____ ; 8. _____ ; 9. _____ ;

10. _____ ; 11. _____ ; 12. _____

4. Recalcitrant consonants 4: missing *p* or *b*

In this text there are ten words which are missing a letter. Five have a *p* missing and five have a *b* missing. However, each of the ten words can take either a *p* or a *b* to make another word, so you have to choose which new word is correct, e.g.: *utter - butter - putter*. Underline each word in the text and write the new word in the list at the bottom.

Harrowing Honeymoon

Last year my fiancé, Rita, and I got married under the trees in our local ark and went on a cruise to New York for our honeymoon. It was a cruise that we will never forget. As a special treat for my new ride, I booked the best suite on the boat. It was really lush, with the most beautiful furniture and decoration you would wish for.

The weather was fantastic for the first week. I took Rita up onto the row of the ship, just like in the film, Titanic, and we stood there with the wind whistling over us.

On the third day of the cruise the captain gave his all. Everyone looked rim in their best clothes at the dance. I'm not the sort of person who goes to these things because I find them a big ore, but I went for Rita's sake. We danced for a couple of hours and then we went up on deck for some fresh air and to look at the stars. Then something seemed to lot out the stars ahead. It was an iceberg, just like with the Titanic! I shouted out loud, but it was too late. The iceberg hit us and reached the hull of the ship, just like a needle would rick a balloon.

Luckily, everyone managed to get in a lifeboat, and the captain sent an SOS to let nearby ships know of our light. We were soon picked up and taken to safety, but we lost everything on the ship, which was a bitter ill to swallow. Still, the main thing was that we had each other and we got to New York after all, unlike the people on the Titanic.

---

1. _____ ; 2. _____ ; 3. _____ ;

4. _____ ; 5. _____ ; 6. _____ ;

7. _____ ; 8. _____ ; 9. _____ ;

10. _____ ; 11. _____ ; 12. _____

5. Recalcitrant consonants 5: extra and missing *s*

In this text there are eight words with an extra *s* and eight words with an *s* missing, all in the initial position. Underline each word in the text and write the new word in the list at the bottom.

___

Sweet and Sour Memories

When you think about your childhood, you usually recall the happy times: the cent of spine trees in the mountains, the feeling of now melting into lush under your feet as spring arrives, your little brother's first mile. I remember my first ride on a team strain; it was absolutely fantastic. At school I remember the first time I tried to write something. It was just a crawl, but my teacher was so pleased that she put a big stick on the page and told me I was smart. I was so proud!

However, sometimes the memories can be bad. Whenever I hear the buzz of a bee I remember the time when I disturbed a warm of them in my garden. I was stung all over, and my smother had to take me to hospital. And what about school uniforms? I used to hate swearing them as I never looked smart. Some of the kids would make fun of me a lot. They used to set straps for me on the way to school and take my dinner money or strip me up when we played football, or even smash my glasses. I also remember I used to bite my snails a lot, and my mother would always cold me for it.

Still, I think there are more sweet memories than sour ones. They're stuck firmly in my mind and they'll always stay with me.

___

1. _____ ; 2. _____ ; 3. _____ ;

4. _____ ; 5. _____ ; 6. _____ ;

7. _____ ; 8. _____ ; 9. _____ ;

10. _____ ; 11. _____ ; 12. _____ ;

13. _____ ; 14. _____ ; 15. _____ ;

16. _____

6. Vagrant vowels 1: missing *a*

In this text there are ten words with an *a* missing. Underline each word in the text and write the new word in the list at the bottom.

A Meal to Remember, or Not

The last time I went to a restaurant I had a really terrible time. I had booked a table for two with my wife at the local Spice Kitchen restaurant, which is a small, net and clean restaurant, just down the rod from our house. However, when we arrived, we saw that all the sets had been taken, so we had to wit another half hour till they had a free table. I went to the toilet to wash my hands, but slipped on some sop on the floor and banged my head.

When we finally got the menu I couldn't red it properly because I had left my glasses at home. I asked the waiter if they had dishes without met, but I think he couldn't her me because the music from the house band was so loud. When he brought the meal, it was wrong, so he had to go back and bring the right one.

When the right meal came, the angry waiter started to put it on the table quickly, but the button on his jacket caught on my wife's necklace and gold chin, which both broke and fell in the food. All the beds from the necklace went into the food. We thought we had got all of them out, but while I was eating, I bit on one and broke my tooth. The pin was terrible! I couldn't eat any more. That was enough for us! We got our cots and left.

---

1. _____; 2. _____; 3. _____;

4. _____; 5. _____; 6. _____;

7. _____; 8. _____; 9. _____;

10. _____; 11. _____; 12. _____

7. Vagrant vowels 2: missing e

In this text there are fifteen words with an *e* missing. Underline each word in the text and write the new word in the list at the bottom.

A Walk on the Wild Side

Last year my brother and I went for a holiday, trekking in the Rocky Mountains in America, and it was a holiday we'll never forget, because I almost did. We mad all our preparations for the trek with our food, drinks, cloths and camping equipment for a week's trip.

The first day was rally lovely - the weather was warm and sunny and the country was fantastic. We walked till sunset and then pitched camp. Even in the summer, the mountains lose hat quickly in the night, so we had to wrap up warm in our sleeping bags.

It was still dark when we woke up. We hard an animal outside the tent. Then it came in the tent and we froze in far; it was a grizzly bar. Before I could do anything, it jumped on me and hit me with its paw. I pulled the sleeping bag over my had but it started to bit me. My brother picked up my walking can and started to bat the animal. Luckily, it let go of me and ran out of the tent.

At first my brother thought I was dad, but then he saw me moving. He managed to call an air ambulance and they took me to hospital. I had serious injuries on my neck and shoulder, but they took good car of me and I flew back to England a couple of weeks later. My only regret is I didn't get any of it on video tap!

---

1. _____ ; 2. _____ ; 3. _____ ;

4. _____ ; 5. _____ ; 6. _____ ;

7. _____ ; 8. _____ ; 9. _____ ;

10. _____ ; 11. _____ ; 12. _____ ;

13. _____ ; 14. _____ . 15. _____

8. Vagrant vowels 3: *i, o, u*

In these sentences there are twelve words with the wrong vowel. In each case, choose the correct vowel from *i, o* or *u*. Underline each word and write the new word at the end of the sentence.

1. I decided to put a new pond in my garden last week, so I dog a big hole, put in plastic sheeting and filled it with water. _____

2. I had planned to take the family out for a picnic today, but it's really cloudy and dill, and it looks like it might rain. _____

3. The two lions fought for a long time before the younger one ran off bleeding from the shoulder to lock his wounds. _____

4. When you use the internet and the computer mouse is on a link, it takes the form of a hand, which means you need to cluck only once. _____

5. After the ship hit the rocks, it quickly took in water through a big hole and started to lust, so the captain decided to abandon ship. _____

6. The government is worried that the most recent opinion pills in the newspapers don't seem to be showing a lot of support for them and their policies.

   _____

7. A lot of parents give their babies a dummy to sock when they start crying, but many dentists think dummies damage gums and growing teeth. _____

8. There's so much traffic and there are so many delays on the roads these days that drivers get angry and are ride to each other a lot more. _____

9. This beach is a great place for a seaside holiday. There's a huge sand done behind here where the children can play every day. _____

10. We used to have a lovely garden until a family of mules moved in. Now they dig new holes in the ground every day. It's really annoying. _____

11. We went horse riding for a week. It was lovely, but my backside was really sure from sitting in the saddle every day. _____

12. While we were walking in the hills, it started snowing, so we were lucky to find a wooden hit where we could shelter for the night. _____

9. Vagrant vowels 4: one vowel too many

In this text there are fourteen words with an extra vowel. Underline each word in the text and write the new word in the list at the bottom.

A Great Granddad

When I was young, I loved visiting my grandfather in the country during the summer. He was such a lovely mane. What I remember moist about him was the big grain that he would have on his face when I arrived. He was always pleased to see me and spoilt me a lot.

He lived in an old house in the woods, a long way from the nearest town, but he preferred it that way. After nightfall we used to sit and look up at the stairs, wondering what it was like to go up there into space. On moonlit nights we'd see lots of mouths flying around as well as the baits that were hunting them.

We would often go for long walks in the woods. He always used a walking canoe because he had injured his leg badly in the ware when he was a soldier. Still, we would walk for miles and site on top of the hills looking into the distance and talking about everything under the sun. We always kept an eye out for wildlife, such as foxes, badgers and deer. It was fascinating to watch the stages with their huge antlers fighting over the does in the autumn. It was the beast time of my life.

Sadly, as he grew older, his leg got worse and he couldn't do things for himself any more. The idea of going into a home would appeal him. Loosing his independence was the last thing he wanted to do, but eventually he realised he needed help, so we arranged for a career to visit him every day and help him. Eventually, when I was twenty-five, he died as he wanted, in his beloved house with his family.

---

1. _____; 2. _____; 3. _____;

4. _____; 5. _____; 6. _____;

7. _____; 8. _____; 9. _____;

10. _____; 11. _____; 12. _____;

13. _____; 14. _____

10. Vagrant vowels 5: one vowel too many

In this text there are fifteen words with an extra vowel. Underline each word in the text and write the new word in the list at the bottom.

A Boy's Best Friend

I'll always remember my dog, Rex. My mother promised me one for my eighth birthday. We went to the local dogs' home, and there were so many looking for a home. In one cage there were five cross-bread Labrador-Alsatian puppies, all jumping and barking, but one joust sat at the back. He looked so acute that I knew he was the one for me.

On the way home in the car he curled up in my leap and fell asleep. When we got home we pout him in his basket, which we had lined with old rages and bits of clothe for him to play with and stay warm. My mum told me I had to take him to be trained, so every Friday we went to training classes. He was a very feast learner.

Every morning he would come and tape on my door and wake me up to go walkies. He loved jumping up to lick me on my chain. I always took him to the park to ruin and chase sticks. He used to love chasing squirrels. As soon as he saw one he shout off after it and he almost caught a few.

When I finished school and went to university I really missed him. Every time I came back he would go made as soon as I walked in the door. As he grew older, he started to get fate and went out for fewer and fewer walks. When I came home from university for the last time, he could barely walk, but he still had that old twinkle in his eye and little wage of the tail, so happy to see me again.

---

1. _____ ; 2. _____ ; 3. _____ ;

4. _____ ; 5. _____ ; 6. _____ ;

7. _____ ; 8. _____ ; 9. _____ ;

10. _____ ; 11. _____ ; 12. _____ ;

13. _____ ; 14. _____ ; 15. _____

11. One way or another 1

Each of these sentences contains a compound word or phrase made up of two words. Each word pair can be reversed to form a compound with a different meaning. Choose one word from the box on the left and another from the box on the right to make the compounds.

| house, shop, shot, song, sore | bird, boat, eye, gun, work |

1. I've always dreamt of living on a canal in a _____ and travelling around the country, so I'm going to buy one next year.

2. I love staying in the peace and quiet of the country. It's so nice waking up to hear _____ first thing in the morning.

3. It's illegal to keep firearms in your house, though farmers can keep a _____ with a licence to control pests, like foxes.

4. I really hate doing _____. It's so boring filling shelves and taking money at the check-out.

5. It's really windy and dusty outside. I've got a really _____. Have you got any drops that I can put in it?

6. My new house is really big. I've even got a _____ where I can make furniture to order for customers.

7. We were walking across the hills when suddenly we heard a _____. Some people were out hunting. We quickly ran into the woods to hide.

8. The first house we looked at was a real _____. The windows were broken, there was rubbish everywhere and the wallpaper was pealing off the walls. No way could we live there.

9. We rented a lovely villa by the river. It even had a really big _____ where we could keep our canoes.

10. Look! There's a thrush singing in that tree. It's a very well-known and popular _____ here in England.

12. One way or another 2

Each of these sentences contains a compound word or phrase made up of the word *back* and another word. Each word pair can be reversed to form a compound with a different meaning. Choose one word from the list to make the compounds with *back*.

| back | date, drop, fire, hand, pay |

1. I checked the hours I've worked and I'm due about £200 in _____ which I didn't get last month. I should get it this month.

2. I got a new pay rise this month, but the great thing is that they decided to _____ it to last September.

3. I've got the use of the college hall for the weekend, but I have to _____ the keys to the office first thing on Monday.

4. Someone in the car shot at the police, so they started to _____. They hit the driver and the car crashed.

5. The location of our holiday home was fantastic. We were right by a lake with the mountains forming a beautiful _____.

6. After about twenty kilometres of the marathon, some runners found the going really heavy and started to _____ through the other runners.

7. This archaeological site is extremely significant. Some of the buildings here _____ to Roman times.

8. The bank said they deposited £2000 into my account by mistake, and I'll have to _____ all of it.

9. When I started my car this morning, it began to _____, so I took it into the garage to check the engine.

10. If you ever have any problems with officials at the passport office, just give them a _____ payment of about £100 and they'll give you a visa on the same day.

13. One way or another 3

Each of these sentences contains a compound word or phrase made up of the word *out* and another word. Each word pair can be reversed to form a compound with a different meaning. Choose one word from the list to make the compounds with *out*.

out	back, break, fall, line, look

1. We thought that our football club had an agreed a deal to buy a new goalkeeper, but the other club decided to _____ at the last moment.

2. The Prime Minister had to resign today after accusations of corruption. The political _____ will be massive, with many changes happening.

3. The first thing I'd like to do at this meeting is to _____ the changes we propose before I get down to talking about the details.

4. When the robbers broke into the bank, they posted a _____ at the front door to check if the police were coming.

5. Here is the evening news. Fifteen children from a school in London have been taken to hospital after a sudden serious _____ of meningitis.

6. Pollution has dramatically increased in the local area because of the waste water _____ from the plastics factory, which goes directly into the river.

7. Recently, our factory's production has increased, sales are rising and we have a skilled workforce, so the _____ for our company is very good.

8. Australia was ideal as a penal colony, because any escaped convicts would find it extremely difficult to survive in the harsh environment of the

    _____.

9. Here is the news. Police are warning residents to stay in their houses following a mass _____ from Bleakmoor Prison. So far only six convicts have been recaptured.

10. There are only two minutes for Manchester to get back into this rugby cup final, so they need to take this _____ quickly and get the ball forward.

14. One way or another 4

Each of these sentences contains a compound word or phrase made up of the word *over* and another word. Each word pair can be reversed to form a compound with a different meaning. Choose one word from the list to make the compounds with *over*.

over	drive, hang, head, look, sleep

1. Although you copied a lot of your project from another student, I'm prepared to _____ it this time, as you admitted it. However, if it happens again, you'll be in serious trouble and lose your place on this course.

2. I've arranged an alarm call in the morning. The flight leaves at 8.00 and we can't afford to _____, or we'll miss it.

3. The climbers examined the cliff carefully. They saw that they could get up most of the way, but the problem was the _____ at the top, which seemed impossible to get over.

4. We were thinking of flying to Germany for the big football game, but it was far cheaper for us all to _____ there in my camper van.

5. OK everyone. The big game starts in an hour, so we'd better _____ to the stadium now to avoid the crowds.

6. The problem that we have is that time is running out to complete this order. We have to get factory production into _____ to do it in time.

7. When you start a new business, you have to carefully consider your _____, like electricity, transport and rent, as well as other costs.

8. Ooh, my head! The party last night was great, but I really drank a lot and I've got a terrible _____. Can you make me some coffee?

9. Can you do me a favour? Could you _____ my history project to check if I've covered everything, before I hand it in to my tutor?

10. I'll have to stay in tonight, as my daughter's having two of her friends round for a _____. It's the first time she's had friends staying for the night.

15. One way or another 5

Each of these sentences contains a compound word or phrase made up of the word *up* and another word. Each word pair can be reversed to form a compound with a different meaning. Choose one word from the list to make the compounds with *up*.

up	keep, set, start, top, turn

1. I had to speak to Jenny for quite a long time. She was very _____ when I told her she didn't get her promotion to the job that she applied for.

2. The call-time on my phone is running low. I need to find a phone shop to get a _____, or I won't be able to make any calls.

3. There are many ways to get money for a business _____, but you have to have a really good business model and plan to show investors.

4. Last year, sales of our raincoats were very slow, but the recent wet weather has meant a massive _____ in sales. We can't sell enough of them.

5. My ex-wife has asked me for more money to help with the children's _____, but I really don't have any more to give her.

6. Nobody expected our team to beat Manchester United, but we fought hard and won. It was a totally unexpected result, a real _____.

7. Jack tries to make out that he's intelligent and knowledgeable, but he actually hasn't got much _____. He's really quite stupid.

8. I went out for a run with the other students at the sports club yesterday, but I found it really hard to _____ with them. I need to get much fitter.

9. I've decided to take the offer of the job. The _____ there is much better than in my company. You can see how well organised they are.

10. I'm really fed up with that little _____. He's worked here for only a month and he thinks he runs the place. He needs to be put in his place.

16. Double-ups 1

Choose one word from each box to make compound words for each clue with the middle word a part of each compound.

out, over, under	cast, come, cover, cut, drawn, dressed, fit, fly, grown, hand, pay, lay	away, back, off, over, out, up

1. This is the result. _____ _____ _____ A performer makes this after retiring from work, and then changing his or her mind and starting again.

2. A cloudy sky. _____ _____ _____ When your ship sinks and you are stuck alone on an island, like Robinson Crusoe.

3. A policeman pretending to be a criminal. _____ _____ _____ A way to stop people finding out the truth.

4. A set of clothes. _____ _____ _____ When the police falsely accuse someone of a crime and create evidence to prove it.

5. Sell products cheaper than your rivals. _____ _____ _____ Something removed from paper with scissors.

6. Too big for your old clothes. _____ _____ _____ Adult.

7. In clothes, too smart for the occasion. _____ _____ _____ With your best clothes on.

8. In a dishonest way. _____ _____ _____ Money given as a benefit to people with little or none.

9. The total amount of money that you spend. _____ _____ _____ Job loss when there's no money to pay workers.

10. Bank account with too much money taken out. _____ _____ _____ Much longer in time than it needs to be, for example, an explanation.

11. Don't give workers enough money. _____ _____ _____ Revenge for something that someone has done.

12. When an aeroplane passes high up. _____ _____ _____ A road which passes over another road.

17. Double-ups 2

Choose one word from each box to make compound words for each clue with the middle word a part of each compound.

out	class, cry, door, gun, house, law, pace, play, post, side	baby, bell, box, breaker, fight, ground, room, setter, ways, wife

1. Perform to a far higher standard than the opposition. _____ _____

   _____ The place where students have lessons.

2. Huge negative public reaction and protest. _____ _____

   _____ Someone who becomes overemotional too easily.

3. Like an activity which is not done in a building. _____ _____

   _____ Ring this to get someone to let you into a house.

4. Have too much firepower for the enemy. _____ _____ _____

   What happens when two gangs shoot at each other.

5. Big building to store things on a farm. _____ _____ _____

   Married woman who takes care of the home.

6. Make something illegal. _____ _____ _____ Someone who

   commits crime.

7. Run too fast for the others in the race. _____ _____ _____

   Someone who runs at the front in a race to make sure the race is fast enough.

8. Perform in a sport to a far higher standard than the opposition. _____

   _____ _____ Where children go to enjoy themselves.

9. A military station on the border of a country. _____ _____

   _____ What you put your letters in to send them.

10. In the open air. _____ _____ _____ Moving neither

    forwards nor backwards.

119

18. Double-ups 3

Choose one word from each box to make compound words for each clue with the middle word a part of each compound.

over	board, book, ground, grow, heat, kill, night, power, weight	bag, case, fall, hog, joy, lifter, point, room, say, wave

1. Where you go when you fall off a boat into the water. _____ _____ _____ Where the company managers meet.

2. Order more tickets than you need. _____ _____ _____ Where you might keep your reading material.

3. What you become if you eat too much. _____ _____ _____ He could also be a bodybuilder.

4. For example, trains which don't go through tunnels. _____ _____ _____ Little squirrel that lives in a burrow.

5. What plants do in untended gardens. _____ _____ _____ You could put young plants in this to start them off.

6. When something interesting reaches your ears. _____ _____ _____ Indirect evidence which can't be used in court.

7. Action which is far more than what's needed. _____ _____ _____ Someone who spoils your fun.

8. Stay and sleep somewhere. _____ _____ _____ The moment the day is over.

9. Attack and subdue. _____ _____ _____ The place in the wall where you plug in an electrical appliance.

10. Leave soup on the cooker too long. _____ _____ _____ Period of very high temperatures.

19. Double-ups 4

Choose one word from each box to make compound words for each clue with the middle word a part of each compound.

back, back, busy, film, foot, gun, motor, night, street, sweet	body, bone, chat, clip, club, dog, heart, hold, home, lamp	all, board, break, fish, head, house, room, shade, sick, work

1. He/she always wants to know what everyone is doing. _____ _____ _____ The metal casing of a car.

2. It runs from your head to your legs. _____ _____ _____ Stupid person.

3. Answering back when someone is telling you off. _____ _____ _____ A place to meet and talk online.

4. A short piece from a movie. _____ _____ _____ It keeps all your papers together and provides base for writing.

5. He/she fetches the bird you've shot. _____ _____ _____ It's like a small shark, but doesn't bark.

6. A place to drink and dance in the evening. _____ _____ _____ Where people drink after playing a game such as golf.

7. It lights the town up at night. _____ _____ _____ You put it on your lights at home.

8. A person you really love. _____ _____ _____ What you feel when a partner leaves you.

9. Somewhere you can place your foot on a climb. _____ _____ _____ A big bag to put your things in.

10. A big van to holiday in. _____ _____ _____ How you feel when you miss your family.

20. Double-ups 5

Choose one word from each box to make compound words for each clue with the middle word a part of each compound.

bath, fun, hand, leg, pass, sign, soft, sound, sun, wheel	chair, fair, port, post, rail, space, sponge, spot, ware, wave	cake, craft, hole, length, light, man, mark, house, way, weather

1. If you can't walk, get around in this. _____ _____ _____ He organises and runs companies and meetings.

2. It carries vibrations through the air to your ear. _____ _____ _____ Every radio station has to be broadcast on one of these.

3. Install and run this on your computer. _____ _____ _____ A big building for storing things.

4. You'll need this to travel abroad. _____ _____ _____ The window out of a ship's cabin.

5. It tells you which direction to go. _____ _____ _____ It tells you when a letter was sent.

6. Room to put your feet on a plane. _____ _____ _____ Something you can leave this world in.

7. Use this to wash yourself all over. _____ _____ _____ Eat this with your afternoon tea.

8. It's a dark place on our star's surface. _____ _____ _____ It shines on the main actor in the theatre.

9. A place for all the family to enjoy themselves. _____ _____ _____ A friend only in the good times is this kind of friend.

10. Hold this when coming down the stairs. _____ _____ _____ What a train runs along.

Grammar Answers

Exercise 1

1. F; 2. P; 3. F; 4. F; 5. P; 6. E; 7. F; 8. F; 9. E; 10. E; 11. E; 12. F

Exercise 2

1. was offered too little; 2. was handed an envelope; 3. were brought our meals; 4. were refused entry; 5. was left over £1m; 6. were promised a saloon car; 7. will be paid double time; 8. I'm (still) owed the other half; 9. was loaned a replacement; 10. will be sent an email

Exercise 3

1. work … am working … aren't running; 2. is always taking … be working; 3. am flying … leaves … arrives; 4. am watching … rings … never answer; 5. starts … am leaving … meeting; 6. is now leaving … hope … arrive; 7. is always working … says … Do … think … is seeing; 8. am thinking … think; 9. am living … save; 10. isn't coming … is studying … is staying

Exercise 4

1. arrived … was … had eaten; 2. were relaxing … heard … had been; 3. finished/had finished … went … danced/were dancing; 4. arrived … was lying … had never seen; 5. was walking … saw … was trying; 6. got … was raining … had brought; 7. had intended … suddenly had … put; 8. told … had bought … saw … was driving; 9. finished/had finished … went; 10. saw … knew … had happened

Exercise 5

1. have been hearing … have heard; 2. have been painting … am getting; 3. have painted … am painting; 4. have called … isn't answering/hasn't answered; 5. have been thinking/have thought … have decided; 6. are still eating … haven't you finished; 7. is shining … has been snowing; 8. is still dating … have been dating … hasn't left; 9. have been expecting … have had; 10. Have … heard … hasn't been working … is leaving

Exercise 6

1. Defining
2. The Prime Minister, who is visiting China this week, has signed a new trade agreement.
3. Defining

4. The audience, who had waited over an hour for the concert to begin, demanded their money back.
5. Another minister has resigned from the government, which is now dangerously close to falling.
6. The leader of the opposition, who accused the Prime Minister of abusing his position, called for a new election as soon as possible.
7. Defining
8. After the game the losing team complained of having to play three times in five days, which had left them absolutely exhausted.
9. Defining
10. The hostages from the hijack were freed by the police and taken to the Central Park Hotel, where they were reunited with their families.
11. My son is really pleased. He managed to get a place at London University, which was the first choice on his application form.
12. Defining

Exercise 7

1. I'm worried about Harry. He's changed so much. He's just not the man ~~who~~ I married.
2. What happened about that job ~~that~~ you applied for? Did you get it?
3. Are you sure that Jenny said that? She's not the sort of person who would gossip about you.
4. Our flat is just far too small now. I'm looking for a large, detached house where all the children can have their own bedrooms.
5. We went skiing over the Christmas holiday. It was lovely. The hotel ~~which~~ we stayed in laid on a really great party for New Year.
6. The only person ~~who~~ I'd give everything up for is my wife.
7. When I told her that she had passed all her exams, she didn't say anything. That wasn't exactly the type of reaction ~~that~~ I had expected.
8. That's the job ~~that~~ I'd love to do, that I'd drop my current job for tomorrow.
9. Is there anyone here who can speak Russian? I can't understand anything ~~that~~ he's saying.
10. There are so many things ~~that~~ I could say about the book that I don't know where to start.
11. The thing which really annoys me about Frank is the way ~~that~~ he talks to other people, as if he were better than them.
12. I don't believe it! I ordered a new computer, but the one which has been delivered is not the one ~~which~~ I ordered.
13. The hotel ~~which~~ we stayed in on this holiday was far better than the one where we stayed last year.
14. The car which is parked outside Pete's house isn't the same car ~~which~~ Pete bought last week.
15. I'd like to know who you think is the best teacher who ever taught you.

Exercise 8

1. along … over/across; 2. past … beyond; 3. over … below … above; 4. above … below; 5. over; 6. across … under … over; 7. below … beyond; 8. over … through; 9. along … past; 10. over … under … above

Exercise 9

1. rear - n; 2. up to now - adv; 3. near - p; 4. motionless - adj; 5. again - adv; 6. here and there - adv; 7. alcohol-making apparatus - n; 8. in the past - adv; 9. stage - n; 10. calmed down - v; 11. circular - adj; 12. support - v

Exercise 10

1. stop - v; 2. quick - adj; 3. rod - n; 4. only - adv; 5. barrier - n; 6. excessively - adv; 7. except - p; 8. eat nothing - v; 9. drinking place - n; 10. also - c; 11. tightly - adv; 12. fair - adj

Exercise 11

1. glass - U; 2. colour - U; 3. a business - C; 4. wood - U; 5. a noise/noises - C; 6. a room - C; 7. glasses - C; 8. business - U; 9. a wood - C; 10. colour/colours - C; 11. room - U; 12. noise - U

Exercise 12

1. experience - U; 2. activity - U; 3. bite - U; 4. deaths - C; 5. colds - C; 6. value - U; 7. a bite - C; 8. activities - C; 9. Cold - U; 10. experiences - C; 11. death - U; 12. values - C

Exercise 13

1. choice - G; 2. a democracy - P; 3. conversation - G; 4. a taste - P; 5. the culture - P; 6. shame - G; 7. democracy - G; 8. a conversation - P; 9. a choice - P; 10. taste - G; 11. a shame - P; 12. Culture - G

Exercise 14

1, discipline - G; 2. A judgement - P; 3. Dress - G; 4. promise - G; 5. the purpose - P; 6. competition - G; 7. a dress - P; 8. a competition - P; 9. a promise - P; 10. judgement - G; 11. a discipline - P; 12. purpose - G

Exercise 15

1. just; 2. sharply; 3. high; 4. close; 5. fine; 6. wrongly; 7. justly; 8. sharp; 9. wrong; 10. closely; 11. highly; 12. finely

Exercise 16

1. short; 2. pretty; 3. lately; 4. hard; 5. easily; 6. free; 7. late; 8. freely; 9. shortly; 10. easy; 11. prettily; 12. hardly

Exercise 17

1. trying - C; 2. trying - A; 3. interesting - A; 4. working - G; 5. working - P; 6. making - P, lying - G; 7. lying - P; 8. joking - C, seeing - G, believing - G; 9. worrying - A, crossing - P; 10. worrying - C; 11. worrying - G; 12. going - G, inviting - A

Exercise 18

1. Saturday ... Thursday ... Friday; 2. the Friday ... the Saturday; 3. a Saturday ... a Sunday; 4. the Monday ... the Tuesday; 5. a Wednesday ... a Thursday; 6. Thursday; 7. Friday ... a Friday; 8. Saturday ... a Saturday; 9. next Wednesday ... the Wednesday after; 10. a Sunday; 11. the Saturday; 12. a Monday

Exercise 19

1. forgot; 2. know about; 3. start; 4. watch for; 5. saw through; 6. apply for; 7. know; 8. start with; 9. forgotten about; 10. apply; 11. seen; 12. watch

Exercise 20

1. allow; 2. engage; 3. arranged for; 4. tried; 5. hit on; 6. bought; 7. buy into; 8. engaged in; 9. allow for; 10. hit; 11. try for; 12. arrange

Vocabareas Answers

Exercise 1

1. lone; 2. loud; 3. live; 4. alone; 5. back; 6. alike; 7. wry; 8. like; 9. broad; 10. aback; 11. aloud; 12. awry; 13. abroad; 14. alive

Exercise 2

1. pace; 2. loft; 3. ashore; 4. breast; 5. head; 6. shore; 7. side; 8. ahead; 9. aloft; 10. aside; 11. apace; 12. abreast

Exercise 3

1. part; 2. wake; 3. asleep; 4. drift; 5. skew; 6. awake; 7. float; 8. aboard; 9. apart; 10. adrift; 11. afloat; 12. askew; 13. sleep; 14. board

Exercise 4

1. inconsiderate; 2. antiseptic; 3. non-event; 4. destabilise; 5. unacceptable; 6. disorder; 7. non-stop; 8. decompose; 9. undesirable; 10. anticlockwise; 11. inflexible; 12. disapprove

Exercise 5

1. non-violent; 2. deregulate; 3. anti-climax; 4. dishonest; 5. irresponsible; 6. unhurt; 7. no-hoper; 8. antivirus; 9. no-go; 10. disqualified; 11. devalue; 12. unattractive; 13. non-stick; 14. impersonal

Exercise 6

1. unsure, insecure; 2. uncomfortable, discomfort; 3. unbelievable/incredible, incredible/unbelievable; 4. unequal, inequality; 5. improbable/unlikely, unlikely; 6. instability, unstable; 7. unjust, injustice; 8. unbalanced, imbalance

Exercise 7

1. unconnected; 2. disinterested; 3. disused; 4. unable; 5. uncover; 6. unaffected; 7. unused; 8. disable; 9. discover; 10. disconnect; 11. disaffected; 12. uninterested

Exercise 8

1. considerable; 2. momentous; 3. apparition; 4. residence; 5. application; 6. populous; 7. momentary; 8. appearance; 9. popular; 10. residency; 11. appliance; 12. considerate

Exercise 9

1. expenditure; 2. publication; 3. government; 4. expectation; 5. reasoned; 6. realism; 7. expectancy; 8. governance; 9. publiclty; 10. expense; 11. reality; 12. reasonable

Exercise 10

1. location; 2. pronouncement; 3. honorary; 4. instant; 5. exposition; 6. instalment; 7. instance; 8. exposure; 9. locality; 10. pronunciation; 11. honourable; 12. installation

Exercise 11

1. ideology; 2. virtues; 3. offences; 4. customs; 5. emotions; 6. senses; 7. behaviour; 8. concepts; 9. skills; 10. vices; 11. penalties; 12. conflict

Exercise 12

1. entertainment; 2. discoveries; 3. disasters; 4. treatments; 5. functions; 6. shelter; 7. institutions; 8. phenomena; 9. inventions; 10. celebrations; 11. events; 12. technology

Exercise 13

1. spices; 2. poultry; 3. beverages; 4. cereal; 5. delicacies; 6. dairy; 7. condiment; 8. produce; 9. spirits; 10. seafood; 11. pulses; 12. herbs

Exercise 14

1. instrument; 2. equipment; 3. ornaments; 4. appliances; 5. material; 6. gadgets; 7. stationery; 8. weapons; 9. hardware; 10. vehicles; 11. tools; 12. utensils

Exercise 15

1. mollusc; 2. wildfowl; 3. primate; 4. shellfish; 5. livestock; 6. amphibians; 7. fauna; 8. predators; 9. vermin; 10. mammals; 11. reptiles; 12. insects

Exercise 16

1. first-hand account; 2. false claim; 3. heated discussion; 4. typical feature; 5. vivid imagination; 6. puzzled look; 7. awkward moment; 8. expert opinion; 9. lukewarm response; 10. nasty shock

Exercise 17

1. crime pays; 2. doubts arose; 3. heart leapt; 4. jaw dropped; 5. mind wander; 6. patience snapped; 7. reputation is growing; 8. rumours were circulating; 9. smile froze; 10. sunlight poured

Exercise 18

1. change course; 2. cheat death; 3. dragging ... feet; 4. cracking jokes; 5. learnt ... lesson; 6. throw ... light; 7. erase ... past; 8. swap places; 9. showing promise; 10. cause ... scene

Exercise 19

1. culture shock; 2. parrot fashion; 3. generation gap; 4. killer instinct; 5. market value; 6. media image; 7. trial period; 8. style guru; 9. sex symbol; 10. safety net

Exercise 20

1. dash ... colour; 2. pile ... junk; 3. couple ... minutes; 4. level ... interest; 5. series ... meetings; 6. volume ... sales; 7. plume ... smoke; 8. member ... staff; 9. host ... stars; 10. grain ... truth

Word Focus Answers

Exercise 1

1. changed hands; 2. change down; 3. loose change; 4. sea change; 5. no change; 6. changeable; 7. small change; 8. change round; 9. for a change; 10. change over

Exercise 2

1. on the receiving end; 2. in the end; 3. ending; 4. at the deep end; 5. split ends; 6. at an end; 7. a sticky end; 8. at the end; 9. on end; 10. no end

Exercise 3

1. end in; 2. ended with; 3. the bitter end; 4. put an end to; 5. end it all; 6. ended up; 7. the end of the world; 8. make ends meet; 9. at my wits' end; 10. to end

Exercise 4

1. windfall; 2. fallout; 3. falls; 4. crestfallen; 5. pitfalls; 6. fall guy; 7. freefall; 8. falloff; 9. rainfall; 10. downfall

Exercise 5

1. falls into; 2. fell about; 3. fell on; 4. fell for; 5. fell away; 6. fell apart; 7. fell to; 8. fell under; 9. falls down; 10. fell out; 11. fell in; 12. fell over

Exercise 6

1. fell to pieces; 2. fell in with; 3. fall ill; 4. fell through; 5. fall into a trap; 6. falling over themselves; 7. fallen foul; 8. fell from grace; 9. fall back on; 10. fell into place

Exercise 7

1. keep-fit; 2. fit up; 3. outfit; 4. fit for; 5. fit in; 6. in fits; 7. good fit; 8. fit to; 9. saw fit; 10. fitting; 11. fit out; 12. have a fit

Exercise 8

1. on his hands; 2. hand in glove; 3. in hand; 4. by hand; 5. on hand; 6. to hand; 7. out of hand; 8. in your hands; 9. hand in hand; 10. off your hands; 11. at her own hands; 12. at hand

Exercise 9

1. hand it to; 2. Get your hands off; 3. keep my hand in; 4. forced my hand; 5. hands are tied; 6. hold your hand; 7. lend a hand; 8. get out of hand; 9. get my hands on; 10. won hands down; 11. have my hands full; 12. turn your hand to

Exercise 10

1. underhand; 2. handed in; 3. hands-on; 4. hand back; 5. handed down; 6. handed on; 7. hand round; 8. hand out; 9. offhand; 10. backhander; 11. handouts; 12. hand over

Exercise 11

1. hand-picked; 2. handbook; 3. handshake; 4. free hand; 5. handmade; 6. handbrake; 7. handwriting; 8. handful; 9. first-hand; 10. handsprings; 11. heavy-handed; 12. handcuffs

Exercise 12

1. hard-working; 2. hard-hearted; 3. hard-pressed; 4. hard-drinking; 5. hard-nosed; 6. hard pushed; 7. hard hit; 8. hard going; 9. hard done by; 10. hard-bitten; 11. hard-hitting; 12. hard-wearing

Exercise 13

1. hard cash; 2. hard shoulder; 3. hard nut to crack; 4. hard disk; 5. hard way; 6. hard sell; 7. hardware; 8. hard labour; 9. hard hat; 10. hard copy; 11. hard currency; 12. hard-headed

Exercise 14

1. hard and fast; 2. hard luck; 3. hardship; 4. harden; 5. hard bargain; 6. took it hard; 7. hard up; 8. hardcore; 9. hard-line; 10. hardy; 11. hard-left; 12. hard of hearing

Exercise 15

1. hit and miss; 2. hit-and-run; 3. hitman; 4. hit on; 5. hit list; 6. hit out; 7. hit song; 8. hit the road; 9. hit home; 10. hit the roof; 11. hit it off; 12. hit back

Exercise 16

1. leasehold; 2. take hold; 3. hold your own; 4. get hold of; 5. holdall; 6. hold together; 7. hold it against; 8. on hold; 9. hold-up; 10. foothold

Exercise 17

1. hold with; 2. holds off; 3. hold down; 4. uphold; 5. hold back; 6. hold on; 7. held out; 8. hold back; 9. hold over; 10. held up

Exercise 18

1. for dear life; 2. life and death; 3. fight for life; 4. for life; 5. larger than life; 6. life worth living; 7. life and soul; 8. fright of my life; 9. new lease of life; 10. for the life of

Exercise 19

1. came to life; 2. live life to the full; 3. risked life and limb; 4. lay down his life; 5. take a life; 6. That's life; 7. have a life; 8. Life goes on; 9. get a life; 10. live my life

Exercise 20

1. life-size; 2. lifelike; 3. lifestyle; 4. lifeblood; 5. life cycle; 6. life forms; 7. lifespan; 8. lifeline; 9. lifebelt; 10. lifetime

Word Groups Answers

Exercise 1

1. one-sided; 2. high fives; 3. one-off; 4. one-and-only; 5. two-timing; 6. one-dimensional; 7. one by one; 8. foursquare; 9. one-way; 10. two-faced; 11. ten a penny; 12. two-way

Exercise 2

1. second; 2. fifth; 3. first; 4. first; 5. second; 6. third; 7. first; 8. second; 9. eleventh; 10. second; 11. sixth; 12. seventh

Exercise 3

1. red; 2. green; 3. blue; 4. white; 5. black ... blue; 6. green; 7. red; 8. blue; 9. red;
10. purple

Exercise 4

1. nudged; 2. sneer; 3. poked; 4. patted; 5. stroking; 6. tapped; 7. scowled; 8.
grinned; 9. squinted; 10. drumming; 11. fidgeting; 12. lit up

Exercise 5

1. recall; 2. recollection; 3. memorise; 4. reminds; 5. memorial; 6. reminisced; 7.
memorable; 8. souvenir; 9. forgettable; 10. forgetful; 11. mindful; 12. amnesia

Exercise 6

1. skimmed; 2. recorded; 3. overwritten; 4. scribble; 5. engraved; 6. scanned; 7.
type; 8. browsing; 9. transcribe; 10. proofread; 11. jot; 12. look over

Exercise 7

1. kneel; 2. perched; 3. crouched; 4. recline; 5. bow; 6. sat up; 7. curled up; 8.
leaning; 9. slumped; 10. cowered; 11. slouch; 12. posed

Exercise 8

1. migrate; 2. tour; 3. hitchhike; 4. ferry; 5. cruise; 6. motor; 7. commute; 8. fly; 9.
voyage; 10. ride; 11. transport; 12. journeyed

Exercise 9

1. lanes; 2. avenue; 3. routes; 4. motorway; 5. flyover; 6. underpass; 7. pass; 8.
tunnel; 9. junction ... lane ... slip-road; 10. roundabout; 11. crossroads; 12. dead-end

Exercise 10

1. correspondent; 2. reviews ... critics; 3. publisher; 4. press; 5. editor; 6. comment;
7. column; 8. article; 9. gossip; 10. periodical; 11. journalists

Exercise 11

1. glacier; 2. jungle; 3. range; 4. archipelago; 5. estuary; 6. channel; 7. desert; 8.
valley; 9. waterfalls; 10. ocean; 11. plain; 12. cliff

Exercise 12

1. ravine; 2. forest; 3. peninsula; 4. continent; 5. plateau; 6. coastline; 7. headland; 8. inlet; 9. volcano; 10. regions; 11. lake; 12. swamp

Exercise 13

1. sales; 2. exchange ... refund ... receipt ... purchase; 3. deposit ... balance ... instalments; 4. order ... discount; 5. cost; 6. value; 7. offer; 8. bargain

Exercise 14

1. hardware; 2. input ... keyboard ... output ... monitor; 3. storage ... hard drive; 4. operating ... upgrade; 5. application; 6. software; 7. log on; 8. processor ... memory

Exercise 15

1. spam; 2. attachment ... virus; 3. download ... upload; 4. blog; 5. firewall; 6. search engine; 7. auction; 8. link ... click; 9. phishing; 10. browser ... surf

Exercise 16

1. downpour ... flooded; 2. breeze; 3. drought; 4. hurricane; 5. heatwave; 6. blizzard ... snowdrifts; 7. gale; 8. depression; 9. squall; 10. humidity

Exercise 17

1. savour; 2. stench; 3. odours (*also* scents *or* aromas); 4. bitterness; 5. scent; 6. stinks; 7. aroma; 8. sniffed ... acrid; 9. whiff (*also* scent); 10. bland; 11. pungent; 12. smacks ... tang

Exercise 18

1. currency ... rate ... exchange; 2. coins ... change ... note; 3. bet; 4. tax; 5. bills; 6. economise; 7. fraud; 8. finance; 9. expenditure; 10. mint

Exercise 19

1. budget ... duty; 2. mercenary; 3. wager; 4. cash; 5. income ... outgoings ... debt; 6. debit ... credit; 7. economical; 8. interest; 9. embezzled; 10. bribe

Exercise 20

1. moisten; 2. evaporates; 3. rinse; 4. drain; 5. brine; 6. condensation; 7. gushed; 8. damp; 9. steam; 10. rainfall; 11. trickle; 12. soak

Word Plays and Games Answers

Exercise 1

1. friction/fiction; 2. fraction/faction; 3. blank/bank; 4. bland/band; 5. clamp/camp; 6. shred/shed; 7. flog/fog; 8. flake/fake; 9. trips/tips; 10. crops/cops; 11. fright/fight; 12. dread/dead

Exercise 2

1. fight/fright; 2. pay/play; 3. gaze/glaze; 4. fee/free; 5. cash/clash; 6. fames/frames; 7. camp/clamp; 8. boom/broom; 9. beach/bleach; 10. band/brand

Exercise 3

1. hilly/chilly; 2. hip/chip; 3. hop/shop; 4. hock/shock; 5. hut/shut; 6. hoe/shoe; 7. hatter/shatter; 8. harp/sharp; 9. hard/shard; 10. hare/share; 11. hat/chat; 12. harming/charming

Exercise 4

1. ark/park; 2. ride/bride; 3. lush/plush; 4. row/prow; 5. ball/ball; 6. rim/prim; 7. ore/bore; 8. lot/blot; 9. reached/breached; 10. rick/prick; 11. light/plight; 12. ill/pill

Exercise 5

1. cent/scent; 2. spine/pine; 3. now/snow; 4. lush/slush; 5. mile/smile; 6. team/steam; 7. strain/train; 8. crawl/scrawl; 9. stick/tick; 10. warm/swarm; 11. smother/mother; 12. swearing/wearing; 13. straps/traps; 14. strip/trip; 15. snails/nails; 16. cold/scold

Exercise 6

1. net/neat; 2. rod/road; 3. sets/seats; 4. wit/wait; 5. sop/soap; 6. red/read; 7. met/meat; 8. her/hear; 9. chin/chain; 10. beds/beads; 11. pin/pain; 12. cots/coats

Exercise 7

1. did/died; 2. mad/made; 3. cloths/clothes; 4. rally/really; 5. hat/heat; 6. hard/heard; 7. far/fear; 8. bar/bear; 9. had/head; 10. bit/bite; 11. can/cane; 12. bat/beat; 13. dad/dead; 14. car/care; 15. tap/tape

Exercise 8

1. dog/dug; 2. dill/dull; 3. lock/lick; 4. cluck/click; 5. lust/list; 6. pills/polls; 7. sock/suck; 8. ride/rude; 9. done/dune; 10. mules/moles; 11. sure/sore; 12. hit/hut

Exercise 9

1. mane/man; 2. moist/most; 3. grain/grin; 4. stairs/stars; 5. mouths/moths; 6. baits/bats; 7. canoe/cane; 8. ware/war; 9. site/sit; 10. stages/stags; 11. beast/best; 12. appeal/appal; 13. loosing/losing; 14. career/carer

Exercise 10

1. bread/bred; 2. joust/just; 3. acute/cute; 4. leap/lap; 5. pout/put; 6. rages/rags; 7. clothe/cloth; 8. feast/fast; 9. tape/tap; 10. chain/chin; 11. ruin/run; 12. shout/shot; 13. made/mad; 14. fate/fat; 15. wage/wag

Exercise 11

1. houseboat; 2. birdsong; 3. shotgun; 4. shop work; 5. sore eye; 6. workshop; 7. gunshot; 8. eyesore; 9. boathouse; 10. songbird

Exercise 12

1. back pay; 2. backdate; 3. hand back; 4. fire back; 5. backdrop; 6. drop back; 7. date back; 8. pay back; 9. backfire; 10. backhand

Exercise 13

1. back out; 2. fallout; 3. outline; 4. lookout; 5. outbreak; 6. outfall; 7. outlook; 8. outback; 9. breakout; 10. lineout

Exercise 14

1. overlook; 2. oversleep; 3. overhang; 4. drive over; 5. head over; 6. overdrive; 7. overheads; 8. hangover; 9. look over; 10. sleepover

Exercise 15

1. upset; 2. top-up; 3. start-up; 4. upturn; 5. upkeep; 6. turn-up; 7. up top; 8. keep up; 9. setup; 10. upstart

Exercise 16

1. outcome - comeback; 2. overcast - castaway; 3. undercover - cover-up; 4. outfit - fit-up; 5. undercut - cut-out; 6. outgrown - grown-up; 7. overdressed - dressed-up; 8. underhand - handout; 9. outlay - layoff; 10. overdrawn - drawn-out; 11. underpay - payback; 12. overfly - flyover

Exercise 17

1. outclass - classroom; 2. outcry - cry-baby; 3. outdoor - doorbell; 4. outgun - gunfight; 5. outhouse - housewife; 6. outlaw - lawbreaker; 7. outpace - pacemaker; 8. outplay - playground; 9. outpost - post box; 10. outside - sideways

Exercise 18

1. overboard - boardroom; 2. overbook - bookcase; 3. overweight - weightlifter; 4. overground - groundhog; 5. overgrow - grow-bag; 6. overhear - hearsay; 7. overkill - killjoy; 8. overnight - nightfall; 9. overpower - power point; 10. overheat - heatwave

Exercise 19

1. busybody - bodywork; 2. backbone - bonehead; 3. backchat - chatroom; 4. film clip - clipboard; 5. gundog - dogfish; 6. nightclub - clubhouse; 7. streetlamp - lampshade; 8. sweetheart - heartbreak; 9. foothold - holdall; 10. motorhome - homesick

Exercise 20

1. wheelchair - chairman; 2. sound wave - wavelength; 3. software - warehouse; 4. passport - porthole; 5. signpost - postmark; 6. leg space - spaceship; 7. bath sponge - sponge cake; 8. sunspot - spotlight; 9. funfair - fair-weather; 10. handrail - railway

www.ingramcontent.com/pod-product-compliance
Lightning Source LLC
Chambersburg PA
CBHW081232090426
42738CB00016B/3270

9 780955 848414